A Meta-Spiritual Handbook

Also by Tim Sledge

Making Peace with Your Past (1992)

Moving Beyond Your Past (1994)

Making Peace with Your Past – South Korea
(1996)

Making Peace with Your Past – Peru (2001)

Goodbye Jesus (2018)

* * *

*Tim Sledge shares insights for growth
on his website MovingTruths.com.*

*For more information on living a meta-spiritual
lifestyle, go to Meta-Spirituality.com.*

A Meta-Spiritual Handbook

*How to Be Spiritual
without Religion,
Faith, or God*

Tim Sledge

Tim Sledge
www.MovingTruths.com.

Debra Wolf, Editor
Cover Design by Natalia Matuszewska

Printed in the United States of America

First Printing: June 2018

Insighting Growth Publications
One Riverway Suite 1700
Houston, TX 77056

www.IGrowPub.com

ISBN-13: 978-0-9998435-9-8 (Paperback)
ISBN-13: 978-0-9998435-8-1 (Kindle E-Book)
ISBN-13: 978-0-9998435-7-4 (Audiobook)

Contents

Part I – How to Be Spiritual Without God

Being Spiritual When Faith Is Gone

Locating the Spiritual in Meta-Spiritual

Comparing Meta-Spirituality to Religion

Sharing My Meta-Spirituality

1 – Being Spiritual When Faith Is Gone

T oday, the only way I can see religious faith is through a rear-view mirror. I don't think any God is listening to any of us or is involved in our lives in any personal way.

In *Goodbye Jesus: An Evangelical Preacher's Journey Beyond Faith*, I shared my story of five decades of up-close involvement with churches, Christians, and ministers. I wrote of what it felt like to be a committed believer and a productive pastor. I did my best to journal my struggles and failures along with my accomplishments. But the heart of the story was my journey out of faith.

The breaking point occurred when I decided that no supernatural source was needed to explain the way of life I had witnessed for decades in one church after another. It all made more sense when I understood that church—as impressive as it could be at times—is just one more human organization. The end of my faith was not far behind.

It might seem surprising, but when my faith ended, I did not stop wanting to be spiritual. I just didn't think it was possible.

Spirituality, in all the forms I'd known, focuses on things that are *beyond* the physical realm and *beyond* normal perception—invisible entities like God, Satan, heaven, hell, and the soul. And faith—not reason—is required to *see* this spiritual realm.

With my new commitment to reason as the basis for my beliefs, I could no longer regard faith as a way to *see* anything. And since faith and spirituality seemed inseparable, I could not imagine how someone like me could be spiritual anymore.

Author David Richo enlightened me. I wasn't looking for a new spirituality paradigm when I read his book, *How to Be an Adult in Relationships*, but that's what I found.

Richo describes himself as "a psychotherapist on a Buddhist path,"[1] and argues that the same attitudes and actions that enable the highest level of human relationships are also the keys to spirituality.

Richo's presentation of spirituality was different enough from my former Christian view that I could relate. And while he pointed to a connection with some larger spiritual force, I felt no pressure to adopt this aspect of his teachings.

The important thing was that Richo's approach gave me hope that I could still be a spiritual person—though in some different way than I had previously imagined. This realization became a launching pad.

The next step was thinking for myself about what spirituality could look like for me—with no belief in God, no buying into any otherworldly concepts, and no credence for some cosmic vibration with which we should all try to be in sync.

You might wonder if my desire to find some workable form of spirituality in my faithless state is a holdover from my past dependence on religion—a sort of methadone to get me through spiritual detox.

I don't think that's the case.

Spirituality continues to intrigue me because I'm still interested in searching for the deepest truths and the highest values in life. I'm still interested in developing my inner life. And I still want to be challenged to be my best self.

After years of following teachings that claimed to be from God, but were actually human in their origins, I decided I would build my own substitute for religious faith.

Why not?

I would come up with my own concept of spirituality.

I just wouldn't claim it was divinely inspired or related to some magical invisible world, or to some mysterious cosmic energy, or to any deity. And I wouldn't promise eternal life, healing, or rebirth.

I decided to use the term "meta-spirituality" to identify my approach as *beyond* any conventional concept of spirituality. I'm not the first person to use this term, and I'm not the first to attempt to define what meta-spirituality looks like. This book is my contribution to a larger, emerging view of secular spirituality.

In the following pages, when I state what meta-spirituality is and isn't, I'm sharing my own opinions. I am writing as one person attempting to redefine spirituality in a way that works for me and hopefully, in a manner that makes sense to others who are seeking to live a meaningful life without God, faith, or religion.

My version of meta-spirituality holds that no existing religion has revealed unmistakable truth about any supreme being. My meta-spirituality rejects the concept of a personal God who is watching over each of us and listening to our prayers. My meta-spirituality also rejects pseudo-scientific mumbo jumbo about connecting with the energy of the universe or getting on the same frequency as some cosmic tuning fork.

You may wonder why I do not abandon the concept of spirituality altogether, and simply pursue the attributes and experiences I seek without calling them *spiritual* in any way. There are two reasons I do not choose such a route.

First, I like the idea of reclaiming, renaming, and redefining the concept of spirituality. There's something pleasing about the thought of being asked, "Are you a spiritual person?" and being able to reply, "No, I'm meta-spiritual." This brings a smile to my face.

But it's more than just giving a concise, thought-provoking description of my new way of living. This reclaiming, renaming, and redefining of spirituality has a higher purpose.

More and more individuals are moving away from religion and religious faith. The fastest growing category in religious preference surveys is "None." This trend might lead us to assume that the topic of spirituality will become less and less relevant. But I don't think that's the case.

There are reasons to believe that many, if not most of us, have an innate interest in—perhaps even a need for—some kind of spirituality.

In this context, it makes sense to seek new options for how we can think of ourselves as spiritual, to redefine an old concept for a new era, and to consider what it can mean to be *meta*-spiritual.

2 – Locating the Spiritual in Meta-Spiritual

Since meta-spirituality does not involve truths revealed by a deity, is not about an invisible spiritual world, and does not require any form of faith, it could be argued that it is not "spiritual" in any sense of the word. But that's a shortsighted view.

Keep in mind that I'm using meta-spirituality to refer to something that is "beyond" any traditional concept of spirituality. Remember that I'm redefining spirituality for a new era. So, it makes sense that this new kind of spirituality will have its own look and feel.

Yet, it is fair to ask, "In what sense is meta-spirituality spiritual?"

Meta-spirituality is concerned with how life can be most meaningful. It looks for the deepest truths and the highest values life has to offer.

Meta-spirituality sees personal growth as a lifelong endeavor and a positive way to live. Meta-spirituality is about finding the best version of yourself.

Meta-spirituality gives emphasis to one's inner life. It is a lifestyle of self-reflection and intentional behaviors that aim to build a core of inner strength.

Meta-spirituality is interested in the quality of human relationships. It fosters a concern about the greater good of humanity. It is keenly interested in the recurring question, "What is the right thing to do?" It is built on values like truthfulness, kindness, humility, gratitude, and generosity.

Meta-spirituality views life as an expectant journey of meaningful experiences, but it is also concerned with how we keep going when life gets tough.

Meta-spirituality is interested in the richness of our emotional lives. It teaches us to rid ourselves of toxic shame, obsessive guilt, and other types of emotional dead weight. And it calls us be fully engaged in life, reminding us of the vital signs of a life that is lived in the present tense: laughter, play, beauty, wonderment, and connectedness.

Finally, meta-spirituality focuses on always remembering that where you are right now—this moment—is the most important place you will ever be, because NOW is when and where life happens. NOW is when and where you find your best self.

3 – Comparing Meta-Spirituality to Religion

What does meta-spirituality look like when you hold it alongside the spiritual practices of traditional religions? Here are a few similarities and differences.

Religious adherents find purpose and meaning in God, his promises, and his plan for their lives. Meta-spiritual people find their own passion, purpose, and meaning in life. Each meta-spiritual person will likely have a somewhat different view as to what provides purpose and meaning.

Religious people get their values from holy books and religious teachers. Meta-spiritual people think about and decide what are the highest and best values for them.

Religious people read and even memorize scripture to remind themselves of the principles by which they seek to live. Meta-spiritual people find multiple sources of insight and motivation. They use affirmations and written core value statements to stay on track.

Religious people pray. Meta-spiritual people think and meditate.

Religious people ask God for guidance. Meta-spiritual people use their minds to seek reasonable insights for direction and truth—wherever such insights can be found.

Religious people ask God for strength. Meta-spiritual people look within for strength.

Religious people confess their sins to God. Meta-spiritual people practice accountability to themselves, to their families, to society, and to selected safe people.

Religious people express gratitude to God. Meta-spiritual people practice an attitude of appreciation without a focus on any divine source.

Religious people worship God, expressing their admiration and devotion. Meta-spiritual people cultivate curiosity about, respect for, and awe of the universe and all that is within it.

4 – Sharing My Meta-Spirituality

At the age of 16, I felt called to be a Baptist minister. I started preaching immediately, pursued my Christian education to the doctoral level, and continued in ministry until I was 53. By the age of 59, at a time in life when many have started ramping up their religious commitment in preparation for their anticipated journey to heaven, I had stopped believing in any kind of religion, faith, or deity.

I no longer view any aspect of my decision to be a minister as a divine calling because I don't believe in the existence of any personal God. But I do believe my adolescent decision to become a minister grew out of a sincere desire to encourage, help, and motivate other people. It wasn't a call from the heavens. It was a call from within that reflected aspects of my personality I was not yet able to consciously identify or explain.

Some former Christian ministers who have left the faith are now "secular ministers" to communities of non-believers. That makes sense to me because I understand still wanting to make a positive difference in the lives of others. It's no longer about being a spokesman for God.

For me, it's about still wanting to facilitate positive change and growth.

What I have to share now comes from my own thinking, insights, and experiences—not from anything perceived as deific in its origins.

I'm writing to inspire, to illuminate, and in some cases, to persuade. I believe in the truth of what I'm writing, and I'm sharing my views on meta-spirituality with conviction and enthusiasm. But I'm also sharing these opinions with a sense of humility.

I don't expect you to agree with me on everything. Some things that matter to me may not matter to you.

I acknowledge your right to make your own choices about meaning, purpose, and values.

I encourage you to receive anything in the following pages that is helpful, and to mentally discard anything that isn't.

Part II – How to See Reality

Seeking Truth Matters

Knowing Yourself Matters

Recognizing Danger Matters

5 – Seeking Truth Matters

The challenge in finding out what is true and what is false is that we often think we know what is real and what is fake when we actually don't.

Our brains more easily accept what we already believe, and struggle to process what conflicts with our existing beliefs. We are likely to place anything that disagrees with our preconceived opinions at the back of the line for consideration. Or, we give those ideas no place in line at all.

We view many things as we were taught to see them when we were children, and early impressions die hard, even when contradictions are staring us in the face. Religion is a prime example when it teaches—during our childhood years—that faith should override reason. Reality is at a disadvantage when competing with these early imprints.

Our human hesitations can cloud reality as well. Some aspects of life may seem too frightening or too painful to accept as real. And when change presses its way into our lives like a slow-moving glacier, our fear of what is different than what we've always known can prompt us to metaphorically pull out a hair dryer, turn it to full heat, and point it at the encroaching mountain of ice. In other words, fear of change can lead to a fight with and ultimately, a denial of reality. You can't melt an iceberg with a hair dryer, but you can try.

Wanting something to be true, needing something to be true, and fearing that the opposite might be what is correct—can all add up to a chosen ignorance of what is accurate, real, and right.

There's strength in numbers, and intentional ignorance grows geometrically stronger in the battle with reality when reinforced by a tribe of other people who think the same way.

We all have tribes, and that's not a bad thing. A tribe can provide a sense of safety and belonging. But if your tribe imposes boundaries on truth, and you refuse to listen to anyone outside your tribe, your thought cage will become an inescapable prison.

Disabling Denial

Denial is the friend of fear, willful ignorance, and backward tribal thinking. Practice denial long enough, and your views will harden like concrete—able to resist the toughest assaults by reality.

The antidote to dysfunctional denials of truth and reality is one of the foundational concepts of meta-spirituality: a bold willingness to follow the truth wherever it leads. And on this truth-seeking journey, science is a great model for how to proceed.

Science shows us how to override our penchant for resisting change to our way of thinking. It teaches us to ask, "What is the evidence that something is true?"

Science begins with a hypothesis, then looks for evidence pro and con. True science follows the evidence—even when it does not point to the desired outcome.

Science teaches us to get comfortable in living with tentative "conclusions" as we continue to take in new information. We cannot stop everything until we know everything, but we can work with the best information we have at any given time, and we can stay open to each new idea, experience, and insight.

And if sufficient evidence is not available, science teaches us that it is okay to say these words: *I don't know.*

Science affirms the value of skepticism, and models not only a willingness to admit it when we don't have enough information to answer a particular question, but also encourages a readiness to say, "I've changed my mind. The position I took a week ago (or a year ago or decades ago) is wrong." Science teaches us to keep reassessing and to keep learning, even when it means changing our minds.

In the beginning, religion filled in the blanks where understanding was lacking. The crops failed because the god of the harvest was angry. A disease outbreak was a punishment from God. A lightning strike was an ominous sign that it was time to sacrifice a virgin.

When science came along, offering better answers for why things happen, the answers were not always welcome. Faith doesn't like competition in pronouncing what's true and what isn't.

In 1633, Galileo was condemned by the Roman Catholic Inquisition for promoting the theory of Nicolaus Copernicus that the sun, not the earth, is the center of our solar system. The Church ordered Galileo not only to stop teaching the concept, but also to stop believing it. More than 350 years later, after a 13-year investigation of Galileo's condemnation, the Vatican admitted he was right.

Although reality is not a choice in a cafeteria line, some individuals and groups consistently choose to say, "I'll have the eyes-closed, my-tribe-knows-best, don't-want-to-look-at-the-evidence casserole. And for dessert, I'll have the everything-is-the-way-I've-always-understood-it pie."

But it doesn't have to be like that.

Open-Minded Thinking

In the meta-spiritual view of things, reality is not a secret. You will not have to choose the right religious book to discover what is real and true. You will not have to locate just the right priest, minister, rabbi, or guru who offers the only pathway to *the* truth. You will not have to pay some person or organization a large sum of money to learn the secret key to life.

But you will have to open your eyes.

Reality and truth are visible to anyone who is willing to examine the evidence, and is committed to do the work necessary to comprehend.

I'm not saying that all truth is simple or easily understandable. Not everyone can master quantum physics or the theory of general relativity. Some areas of knowledge are hard to grasp even if you're a specialist, and there's too much information now accessible for any one of us to know everything.

But I am saying that the basic truths about what's real and what isn't are not secrets available to only a select few.

Often, it's not that truths are beyond our grasp, it's that we're committed to the blinders we wear, and we don't want to take the time to stop and think about what we believe we already understand.

Meta-spiritual thinking is open-minded and expectant— always ready to learn something from even the most unlikely person, place, or thing. It's an attitude that looks forward to each new discovery whether the source of the insight is ordinary or surprising.

Looking Deeper

Another lesson from science that is helpful in our search for truth is the value of looking deeper. Biology tells us that we are not just skin and bones. We are made of trillions of tiny cells. With microscopes, MRIs, CAT scans, and a myriad of other tools, we can now look deeper to see the parts inside that make us work.

Physics tells us that the cells in our bodies are made of atoms with protons, neutrons, and electrons inside. Partnering with astronomy, physics tells us that stars are beyond what we can imagine in both their size and distance. Black holes can't be seen just by gazing, but science finds ways to *see* the invisible.

Science teaches us to look deeper.

A key element of the meta-spiritual mindset is that what something initially appears to be is simply the most visible part of a more complex reality. We can discover more of the truth about things—and people—when we live with the awareness that all around us there is more than initially meets the eye.

Consider a dining room table. When you look at it, you see a stationary, solid object. Although it looks solid, the table actually consists of millions of atoms with electrons whirling around at staggering speed. Between the electrons and the nucleus of each atom are microscopic—but proportionately huge—open spaces. Despite appearing solid, the dining room table is more empty space than anything else.

And that's not all. The table appears to be standing still, and, as an observable thing in the dining room, it is standing still. However, not only is it crammed full of zooming electrons, it's in a room on a planet that is spinning at 1,000 miles an hour while orbiting the sun at 67,000 miles an hour in a solar system circling the center of the Milky Way at over 400,000 miles an hour.

The dining table appears to be a solid object that is standing still, and it is, but it isn't.

Meta-spirituality calls us to a deeper look at everything that surrounds us. Looking deeper means learning and thinking about the microscopic world we cannot see, and it means we are curious about what is light-years away.

And if something as simple as a wooden table is so much more than what it appears to be, then what about people? Each person is complex, and not just in their physical makeup. Every person has a unique story. There's much more to every individual than meets the eye.

Meaningful connections with other people require a desire to look deeper—a passionate curiosity, a willingness to listen, and to care about what we learn. We discover the truth about individual human beings as we ask about and listen to their stories.

As we refine our skills for looking deeper and listening

better, we are able to learn more—and to connect more significantly with the world and the people in it. And soon we will find ourselves living life at a deeper level, more capable of taking in the richness of it all.

Thinking things through, using our common sense, seeking balance, applying our core values, weighing the psychological implications—all these tools apply as we make decisions about what is true or false, good or not so good, real or fake.

The alternative: Living without an openness to learning, change, and growth will harden you into a brick made only of things accepted long ago and never reviewed or questioned. When you are a metaphorical brick, the ever-learning and ever-changing world will pass you by.

Meta-Spiritual Principle

Seeking Truth Matters: Look deeper, be willing to change your mind, and follow the truth wherever it leads.

This principle applies to all kinds of truth: facts about the physical world, understanding what's real and what isn't, deciding what really matters, discovering what makes other people who they are, and understanding yourself.

6 – Knowing Yourself Matters

The hardest thing to see—is me. It's hard to find the highest and best in life when you don't have an accurate understanding of yourself. It's not possible to become your best self if you don't know who you are.

Self-awareness requires more than a glance in the mirror. In fact, it's hard work. Socrates is reported to have said, "The unexamined life is not worth living." Robert Fulghum added, "The examined life is no picnic."[2]

The journey of knowing yourself is a challenging one, especially at first. To fully comprehend the ins and outs of who you are, you will likely need to be willing to feel worse before you feel better. But it's worth the work and discomfort.

Knowing yourself is empowering, and it's a crucial element in our meta-spiritual quest to find truth—to understand things as they really are.

Looking deeper applies not only to the entities and people around us. It applies to looking at yourself as well.

Discovering Blind Spots

When driving a car, it's hard to see the spot just behind you on the passenger side. It's called a "blind spot" because even with a neck-craning look and a glance at all your mirrors, you may miss a car lurking just behind you and to your side.

Some vehicles now offer an electronic "blind spot checker" that lights up in the side-view mirror when there is a vehicle hiding—or sometimes speeding through—your blind spot.

Too bad we don't have some type of personal blind spot alert app—one that can read your brain and output a warning to your smartphone. Until such an app exists, we'll have to do our own work at finding our blind spots.

However big or small, whatever your blind spots look like, knowing what they are and addressing them will help you grow. What you don't know *can* hurt you.

Discovering and understanding a blind spot can make you aware of something about yourself that other people figure out within minutes of meeting you.

Not knowing who you are slows you down in life—like moving through a dimly lit room rather than one in which the lights are fully turned up.

Our blind spots are often hiding places for character flaws—areas that need work, but are painful to face. And you could have a blind spot for some gift or talent you possess, a trait that is hidden from you, but obvious to others who know you well. Wouldn't that be nice to know and to use to your advantage?

Keep in mind that sometimes blind spots take cover behind our best traits. For example, you're intelligent, even gifted—that's positive—but your blind spot is that you tend to assume you're always right in a way that comes across as arrogance. Or, your kindness is what people love most about you—definitely a positive trait—but your blind spot is that you are sometimes kind in a way that allows others to take advantage of you.

Finding your blind spots is not something you do alone. You need help—that's why they're called blind spots.

You can look in your own meditative mirror all you want and still miss a blind spot. It's beneficial if you have a loving friend, relative, or partner who's shared innumerable experiences with you, has no ax to grind, is not jealous of you nor condescending, and, is as courageous and honest as they are kind.[3]

Once you have identified a trusted individual who can help you see yourself better, you'll need to convince this blind spot revealer that you are ready to listen to whatever you need to hear and that you won't attack the messenger.

"Tell me something I don't know about myself" is a good place to start. Or, maybe you have a hunch about a blind spot of yours, and want to be more specific in what you ask, for example, "Do you think I have a problem with x?"

It may take some coaxing to get your potential mirror person to tell you what they really see, and how you respond to his or her first comments will likely determine the extent and honesty of further feedback. So, brace yourself and plan your response. "Thank you for your feedback," is a good reply.

If you think what is being said is not accurate, apply extra effort toward open-mindedness, keep listening, and ask clarifying questions. Is the person providing feedback someone who truly cares about you and has no hidden agenda? Does this person know you well? Is this someone who you generally regard as insightful? If the answer to all these questions is yes, seriously consider what this person is telling you.

If one item of feedback is all you're ready to hear, clearly communicate your desire to stop. "Thank you for your feedback. I need some time to process it."

Your internal response to the feedback could be an immediate recognition of its truth. You sort of knew it before you heard someone else say it, and hearing it from a person who cares about you simply makes it more real.

Or, the feedback could be a total surprise like the blaring horn you hear when you start pulling into the next lane with a car in your blind spot. If the information catches you off guard, don't panic—and don't immediately assume it's true or not true.

If you doubt the accuracy of the feedback you've received, go to a second person who meets the same criteria as the first: has shared multiple and varied experiences with you, no ax to grind, not jealous, not condescending, kind, honest, and courageous.

Here's a good intro for your second blind spot feedback conversation. "I'm on a reflective journey—trying to understand myself better—and I'm working to learn more about myself and make some improvements. I've gotten feedback from one person, and I'd like to bounce it off you." Be sure you don't say, "You don't think I have a problem with (whatever the first person said about you), do you?"

What's important is to choose someone who is kind but also sees more value in telling you the truth than in making you feel good in the moment. If you've picked the wrong person, he or she may tell you what you want to hear—even while knowing the feedback you received from your first conversation was, in fact, true.

Your spouse or life partner may have been alerting you to one or more blind spots for a while, and a new openness to his or her previous input could be a good starting place. Your partner may be your best source of feedback if you can be open and vulnerable enough to hear, and can do so without retaliating.

There are many reasons for *not* asking your children to tell you what your blind spots are. An especially mature older teenager might be ready and able, but be careful. Caution is in order any time someone who is not yet an adult is expected to take on an adult role. Don't create a situation that will be awkward for both of you after difficult words have been spoken.

An adult son or daughter could be one of your best sources for honest feedback, but you must be determined to not let what an adult child tells you hurt your relationship in any way. Don't punish the messenger even if the message is inaccurate or not what you want to hear.

Whoever your feedback person is, be sensitive to their need for personal boundaries. Communicate that you want him or her to be comfortable with the conversation, and be sensitive to the possibility that she or he may be ready to give you feedback in certain areas, but not in others.

Only you can decide if the feedback you receive about yourself is accurate. Be careful about discrediting similar messages from multiple people who know you well and care for you deeply—they are likely to contain some truth.

If you're tempted to declare yourself blind spot free, be careful, because one of the reasons we have blind spots is denial.

Dealing With Denial

Simon Cowell was notorious for excoriating contestants who showed up to try out for the *American Idol* television show even though they were absolutely awful singers. It happened so often that you could anticipate the disbelief, the shattered look, and the process of turning on the judges by the contestant who simply could not sing a note.

Clearly, prior to the audition—and possibly even afterwards—the aspiring vocal star on the receiving end of Cowell's derision really believed they could sing like an angel. This is a perfect example of denial.

These professional singer wannabes were likely failed by friends and loved ones who thought it better to help them feel they were good at something rather than telling them the truth: You can't sing, and you need to try something else.

When you receive false information about who you are and what you're good at—especially from one or more key people in your life—if it goes on long enough, it may be very hard to stop believing what you've been told. This can be the case even when it's obvious to just about everyone else that what you believe about yourself is not true.

Denial is the head cheerleader for our blind spots.

Denial stares truth down daily. Denial protects us from hearing what we do not want to hear and seeing what we do not want to see.

Why would anyone want to live in denial? Here's one motivation: fear of the feelings that will follow if you face the truth.

Knowing What You Are Feeling

Our need to maintain blind spots and stay in denial may be connected to an unwillingness to acknowledge and experience each of the emotions that come our way. It's natural to resist pain, but fear of experiencing emotional pain can become a detrimental driving force.

Turning your back on your emotions empowers and energizes them for a long-running attack on you.

This truth became more real in my life in 1988, when I spent five days at The Meadows, a recovery facility in Wickenburg, Arizona. I went there to gather material for a sermon series, but ended up doing work as an adult child of an alcoholic.

It was a life-altering week of small group therapy, and the question I heard over and over was, "How does that make you feel?"

At first, I'd answer with something like, "I think the situation I'm in is a difficult one." The group leader would respond, "You didn't answer the question. How does that make you feel?"

My answers were sourced from thinking rather than feeling. My group leader was working to help me zero in on one or more basic emotions—shame, guilt, anger, sadness, fear, pain, loneliness, peace, or joy.

After a few days in the group, I started to get the hang of it, but it wasn't easy. I learned better, more accurate answers like, "I'm feeling sad right now," or "I feel angry about that," or "I'm feeling joy."

In those few days, I learned that I had spent a lifetime shelving away many of the emotions inside me. That week, I learned to say no to the fear of acknowledging what I was feeling and to embrace even my negative emotions. I learned that when I embraced a downbeat emotion, when I gave it a voice, I reduced its power, and could more easily let it go.

And I learned that a key aspect of emotional health is being able to identify what you are feeling at a given moment.

If you are feeling angry, it is good to be in touch with that, to think about why you are angry. If you are feeling shame, it is good to be able to admit that, and to reflect on where the shame is coming from. If you are feeling joy, but cannot acknowledge it, that's an issue to overcome, and the starting point in overcoming is asking "Why?"

Becoming willing to feel your emotions—whatever they are—empowers you to break out of the prison of denial to see your blind spots, to accept what needs to be accepted, and to work on changing what needs to be changed. Embracing your pain allows you to let it go.

Looking Deeper

Discovering our blind spots is just one way we can know ourselves better. Reading about issues we face, participating in support or therapy groups, and one-to-one counseling are other ways we grow in self-awareness.

Meta-spirituality is a call to introspection, a belief that looking deeper within is the only way we will ever see our true selves—and since we are constantly evolving and reacting to new experiences, as we look inward, we are not looking at a stationary target.

This means that we need to get comfortable with an introspective lifestyle and learn to regard it not like a painful root canal—something you just want to be over with—but rather, as a good way to live life.

Seeing introspection as a normal part of an emotionally healthy life does not mean you should head for a monastery and spend every waking hour in introspection. It does not mean you are selfish, self-absorbed, or narcissistic. On the contrary; one of the intended results of knowing yourself is how this awareness can positively affect your interactions with other people—including giving you the freedom to respond to the needs of others in a sensitive way. So, if introspection is all you do, you're doing it too much.

Meta-spiritual growth occurs as you learn more about your own uniqueness, history, strengths, weaknesses, unresolved issues, and even your dark side, the other "you" that appears under stress. This growth takes place as you move beyond the fear of experiencing your emotions and become more willing to see yourself as you really are.

Curiosity turned inward leads to self-awareness, and self-awareness is at the core of what it means to be meta-spiritual.

Meta-Spiritual Principle

Knowing Yourself Matters: Never stop learning about who you are—even when doing so is painful or challenging.

7 – Recognizing Danger Matters

This world is not a safe place. In fact, it's downright dangerous. When I was an evangelical Christian, I had a simple explanation: Adam and Eve succumbed to Satan's temptation, and by their choice, brought sin into the world.

My Christian frame of reference led me to think as follows: Because of the disobedience of Adam and Eve, the world became a dangerous place where suffering and death are possible. Every person born after this *fall of man* inherits a nature inclined toward sin and susceptible to temptation. Satan is still active in the world—an ongoing spiritual battle is in progress—and evil increases when individuals give in to his temptations. Human suffering is the result of living in a fallen world where one's own sinful choices and the sinful choices of other people cause pain and loss. The fall in Eden also disrupted the natural order of things, creating an unsafe physical world where natural disasters can occur.

Today, simply describing these ideas I once regarded as true is a source of embarrassment. But when I abandoned my simplistic belief in the existence of Satan and decisions made in a primordial garden, I was left with a disconcerting void. Why do people rob, rape, and murder? Why do people abuse children? Why do some people get joy from inflicting pain upon others? Why are some people evil?

Even without my Christian belief system, even with my new commitment to find reality through reason, I had to admit that evil is real and ever-present. Human-against-human actions damage and destroy lives every single day.

Based on 2015 averages, in the next hour or so in the U.S., 10 individuals will be raped and two people will be murdered.[4] The sad list of horrific ways people hurt each other goes on and on: child pornography, human trafficking, sex slavery, torture, serial killings, and genocides.

We need locks on our doors. Fear causes many to arm themselves. We must protect our Social Security numbers and our credit cards. We are on guard against identity theft. Bank tellers in major cities work behind bullet-proof glass. We walk through metal detectors before we can board an airplane.

If we watch too much news, we might decide that any feeling of safety is an illusion.

If there is no Satan waging spiritual warfare against humanity, how do we explain all the ways that humans hurt and kill one another? What is the reason for so much suffering and evil?

If we are not stained by the sin of a mythical Adam and Eve, then what makes individuals—even groups of people—do terrible, hateful, and harmful things, sometimes falling into a pattern of acts so unthinkable that we must call such behavior evil?

No simple answer exists. However, since meta-spirituality is about seeking truth and wanting to understand things as they really are, this is an important topic.

Human behavior is complex, and human actions have multiple, often complicated causes. Every single event that occurs is affected by millions of events that precede it.

Sometimes good people do bad things, and a small percentage of people are so malevolent that it's hard to see any good in them.

I don't know all the reasons, and I'm not sure anyone has a full explanation. Nonetheless, here are some non-supernatural causes for humans behaving badly—in no particular order.

Animal Instinct
We are evolved animals. A primitive survival instinct resides just below our conscious thinking.

This animal nature can be unleashed when our basic human needs for air, water, food, shelter, or safety are not being met. A part of us is designed to fight to stay alive.

When our very existence is at risk and we feel that our options for survival are limited, we may act like a cornered animal.

On the other end of the spectrum, our baser nature can emerge if we become extremely powerful—with access to wealth and influence or dominance in military conflict. If your moral guidelines are not able to hold the line, power can "go to your head" in a way that deadens your capacity for empathy, and leads you to act like an alpha male beast.

Some of what we call evil happens when animal instincts prevail over the more evolved parts of the human brain.

Mental Health

The brains of some individuals don't work properly when it comes to making decisions about appropriate behavior.

In *The Sociopath Next Door*, Martha Stout, a psychologist who spent decades studying sociopaths, writes that about one in 25 people in the U.S. is a sociopath.[5]

A sociopath lacks empathy and remorse. Fear of punishment, not conscience, is the sociopath's motivation for following the rules and laws of society—that is, if they follow the rules. They feel entitled, and will lie to get what they want. A sociopath can be very charming, but it's an act, and the goal is manipulation and control. A sociopath may be incapable of love, is driven by hostility, and is likely to seek revenge.

A vast quantity of human suffering can be traced to the actions of sociopaths—the more power and influence they wield, the more damage they are likely to do.

Sociopathy is but one example. Only a small percentage of individuals with mental illness commit violent acts, but psychotic episodes, paranoid delusions, affective disorders, delirium, dementia, post-traumatic stress, intermittent explosive disorder, sexual sadism, and antisocial personality disorder can be contributing factors. In addition, human behavior can be dramatically affected by a chemical imbalance in the brain.[6]

There are so many ways a malfunctioning brain can lead to doing harm to others. And, some forms of mental illness drive an individual toward self-harm, including suicide, that triggers a damaging ripple effect, inflicting deep suffering on friends and family members.

Substance Abuse

The misuse of ingested substances causes untold loss, suffering, and death. Some 88,000 people die each year in the U.S. from alcohol-related causes alone, and according to the National Institute of Alcohol Abuse and Alcoholism, in 2015, 15.1 million adults 18 or older had an alcohol use disorder.[7]

Substances like cocaine, methamphetamines, and heroin destroy human lives. Prescription drugs can be misused in deadly ways. The opioid crisis is raging, and no one seems to know how to curb it.

Read today's newspaper for examples. It doesn't matter where you live or what day it is. Who could imagine one edition of a newspaper that does not contain some notice of a loss triggered by alcohol or drug abuse?

The damage done by substance abuse is not limited to a driving arrest or a hit in the face or an accident or a gunshot. Relationships can be severely damaged or ended by the emotional injuries dealt by persistent substance abuse. Relatives who are addicted weigh heavily in the concerns of those who love them—often for a lifetime.

Hurt People

The boss yells at Dad because he lost a big contract. At home, Dad yells at Mom, not really because of anything she did, but because the boss yelled at him. Mom, hurt by Dad's outburst, scolds little Jimmy for some random thing he forgot to do. Jimmy feels hurt, so he gives the family cat a kick off the sofa. When someone is hurt, the pain can cascade down through a network of innocents.

When it's more than a passing emotional wound—when, for example, a child is the direct victim of abuse—the damage is more than an uncomfortable moment. The pain becomes chronic, and there are many ways the hurt may be passed on.

Contrary to conventional wisdom, most abuse victims

don't become abusers, but it's easy to pass the pain along in other ways. Later in life, the abuse victim's partner may feel pain in the victim's inability to trust—even when trust has been earned. Family members may be pulled down by the chronic depression of a parent abused long ago, but still hurting. When things feel out of control during childhood, we may develop a need to be in control—of everything—and that's not pleasant for those who intersect our paths.

But sometimes childhood abuse is like the mythical vampire bite where the victim becomes the predator who then inflicts the wound on someone else. And childhood abuse can lead to acting out in other ways besides perpetrating the abuse received early in life. One study indicates that the U.S. prison population has about twice the number of victims of child abuse as compared to the general population.[8]

A similar scenario can take place on a societal level. One nation starts a war. The other side doesn't want combat, but must protect itself, so it fights back. Soldiers on the defensive side are primed to inflict additional pain and suffering on their attackers when they see fellow soldiers killed, injured, or find that torture has occurred. What follows is death on both sides—including non-combatants, adults, and children—so-called collateral damage.

Hurt people, because of their own pain, often—in many different ways—hurt other people. And all these actions add up to become part of the sum of pain, suffering, and evil in the world.

Flawed Leadership

Human behavior is affected by the moral quality of human leaders. Leadership affects families, businesses, cities, and nations. If we are being led by an individual who constantly feels threatened or was severely abused as a child and has not dealt with the impact of that abuse, if we are being led by an active substance abuser, if we are being led by someone who is mentally ill in a way that conscience is switched off or there is a reality disconnect, we're in trouble.

And it's not just that seriously flawed leaders *lead* badly. People who follow flawed leaders sometimes do things they would never consider doing on their own. We have only to consider Scott Peck's example in *People of the Lie*, where he describes how some U.S. soldiers in Vietnam succumbed to a group mentality that sanctioned inhumane treatment of innocent civilians. Individual soldiers committed atrocities they would never have perpetrated on their own—because of bad leadership.[9]

Impersonal Universe

Human beings are not the only cause of terrible events that cause pain and suffering. Natural disasters like tornadoes, hurricanes, floods, famines, wildfires, and earthquakes touch the lives of millions of people every year.

If you are a multi-millionaire, a rock star, or a top professional athlete, it may be easy to think the universe loves you, especially if you are cocooned in a beautifully secure and privileged lifestyle. However, if you are a starving or abused child, you might not be so receptive to this idea.

Let's say that the universe isn't evil, it's just impersonal. The universe operates according to its own natural laws. It doesn't hate you or love you. The universe is indifferent about what happens to any of us.

If you jump out of a plane without a parachute, you'll find that gravity is uninterested in your well-being—it will do what it does—and pull you down to your death.

If you leap off an ocean liner in the middle of the night hundreds of miles from land, you'll find that the water is not concerned about your survival. If you survive the impact, when you get too tired to swim, the sea will swallow you.

If you hitch a ride on a spacecraft, and step outside without a spacesuit, the vacuum of space will be apathetic about your death. It will suck the air out of your lungs and freeze you in an instant.

The universe is indifferent toward you and me, and is the source of many of the destructive, terrifying, and most challenging events we humans must face.

Situational Awareness

So, how do we deal with the fact that human suffering results from bad, sometimes evil, acts by other people and is also caused by the impersonal forces of nature?

This question is made more acute by the fact that no personal God is watching over us—which means we may not always be safe—and by the fact that this life is all we have—which makes staying alive even more important.

Religious people say that everything happens for a reason. Even when something really dreadful happens, they say, "Don't worry. God is using this terrible event in a way to bring about something good in your life." And if some horrible event brings your life to an untimely end, faith is still there, promising a better life after this one.

Meta-spirituality posits that everything happens for a million reasons, and recognizes that survival is not guaranteed. Sometimes bad things happen, and all we can do is try to survive, and if we do stay alive, attempt to learn from what we experienced.

This dose of reality is not meant to be a downer, and it need not lead to despair. It simply means that we need to practice situational awareness. The world is a dangerous place.

We need to protect ourselves from individuals and groups who would do us harm, and we should not be naïve about weather, climate, and the environment.

It makes sense to link ourselves with people who are kind and good, and to join with such people in looking out for one another and for the people in our lives who are fragile, frail, or vulnerable.

Meta-Spiritual Principle

Recognizing Danger Matters: Don't give in to fear, but be realistic about life's dangers. Do what you can to protect yourself and others from harm.

Part III – How to Live With Meaning

Present Tense Matters

Relationships Matter

Values Matter

Purpose Matters

8 – Present Tense Matters

It's hard to learn from the past if you don't reflect on it from time to time. If there's pain in your past, embracing the pain is a step toward letting it go—and that means thinking about the events that created the pain. Telling our children and grandchildren stories from the past is a way of passing along the wisdom we have acquired. And when we lose a loved one, part of the grief process is remembering. There are times when we need to focus on the past.

Only a foolish person never thinks about the future. Planning ahead is a way of taking responsibility for your life whether it's thinking about a job change, planning a vacation, or buying an insurance policy. Visualizing how you would like your life to look in the future is a step toward improving, growing, and moving forward.

While supporting the value of reflecting on the past and planning for the future, meta-spirituality focuses on always remembering that where you are right now—this moment—is the most important place you will ever be, because NOW is when and where life happens.

We can miss out on life by focusing too much on regretting past events or worrying too much about what might happen in the future. And even when we're not thinking about the past or the future, we can still be "somewhere else" in the present moment. There are a million ways to be "miles away" while in the presence of an important event or personal interaction.

Since now is when and where life happens, it's important to be fully engaged in the current moment, to live—as much as possible—in the present tense.

As with the options for being "somewhere else," there are countless ways to engage with the present moment. But some types of experiences demand our present-tense participation—I call them *conscious participation required* experiences. Some examples are: laughter, play, beauty, wonderment, and connectedness.

When a *conscious participation required* experience is in progress, it's hard—virtually impossible—to be somewhere else mentally. These are experiences that pull your consciousness into the present moment and have a way of resuscitating you when you've fallen into a rut of disengaged living. I like to think of them as *CPR* experiences.

A good self-check for how often you are showing up for the present moment is reviewing the last few days, weeks, or months for the presence—and recurrence—of moments of laughter, play, wonderment, and other *conscious participation required* experiences.

Laughter

Sneezing and laughter are both spontaneous physical events that are hard to stop once they start. Sneezes are cleaning-out events. The purposes of laughter are harder to define, but one thing is certain—laughter is a *conscious participation required* experience.

The importance of laughter is evidenced by the fact that great comedians are paid large sums of money to make us laugh, while—at least as far as I know—no one gets paid to make us sneeze.

Laughter can take on a dark side when it is derisive and mocking, but most of the time, laughter is a positive event.

How long has it been since your last belly laugh? How long since you couldn't stop laughing? Do you laugh often? What are your dependable sources for generating laughter? Are you too serious too much of the time?

Play

Children play; animals play; and adults should play too. We pay to watch others play with skill—football, basketball, baseball, soccer, and more. But we should engage in our own play, the kind where skill doesn't matter and winning is not the objective.

There are a million ways to play. Playing is doing something that feels good, but doesn't necessarily have a purpose—other than playing. It's a way of disconnecting from life's routine and engaging with the present moment. It's a way of acknowledging there's more to life than winning, working, eating, and sleeping. Play bridges barriers: age, ethnicity, gender, and sometimes even species.

When was the last time you played, not to win, but just for the sake of play?

Beauty

In the philosophy of religion, the existence of beauty is argued to be one of the proofs that God exists. But even without faith, the fact that we can conceive of anything as beautiful points to a hard-to-define and somewhat mysterious part of life.

Beauty gets your attention, pulls you toward it, and draws you into the now—conscious participation is required.

We are enthralled and uplifted by beautiful scenery, paintings, music, and other forms of art. We can't help but notice beautiful people, and we are likely to be biased in their favor, at least initially, even if we're a bit jealous.

There's something about beauty that we all understand. When someone describes an experience as a "beautiful moment," we may have questions as to exactly what happened, but we understand that something wonderful has occurred.

Life without beauty is life in survival mode.

Wonderment

A sense of wonderment is part of what we may feel in the presence of beauty, but wonderment is about more than beauty. It's about how we respond to the magnitude and mystery of life.

When I left my faith, I didn't lose my sense of wonderment—in fact, my capacity for wonder grew. My old approach was pretty much "Isn't God great." After leaving faith, I began to read and learn more about physics, astronomy, and evolution. As my understanding of these fields of study grew, so did my capability to experience wonderment at the magnificent complexity of existence. I also became more aware of how much I do not and cannot know, which added to my sense of wonderment.

Whatever the source—a starry night, a spectacular view, a rocket pushing into space, a newborn baby, a captivating painting—when you are experiencing wonderment, you are in the present moment.

Meta-spirituality is the opposite of a ho-hum approach to life. It cultivates an attitude that is on the lookout for anything that evokes a sense of wonderment.

Connectedness

Another vital sign of an emotionally rich, fully engaged life is connectedness—connections to people, events, and ideas.

When we are distracted, disengaged, and isolated—that's the opposite of connectedness.

The desire to be a spiritual person includes a longing to be connected with something beyond yourself, but that doesn't have to be deity.

When a crowd laughs together, it is connected.

When I play with one of my grandchildren, we are connected.

Friends hiking a wilderness trail and enjoying the beauty of nature together are connected.

When you gaze at an eloquent work of art in a museum, you are connected to its beauty and its message.

When you look at the stars in wonder, you are connected to the mystery of existence.

When you sit in an audience enthralled by an inspirational speaker, you are connected with the speaker, other members of the audience, and with a vision of how life could be better than it is.

When you are having an open, honest conversation with another person, you are connected not just by the words being spoken, but by some deeper bond.

There is an aspect of connecting in these ways that allows

us to feel we are part of something outside of, bigger than, and more than ourselves.

When we are connected, we are in the present moment.

Vital Signs

Conscious participation required experiences are the vital signs of an emotionally rich, fully-engaged, present tense life. You're less likely to see them when death is near. They're harder to find when you are depressed or under the control of fear.

So, when you feel like you are dying emotionally, when you are weighted by depression, when your fears are haunting you, look for a CPR experience. Look for the resuscitation of laughter, play, beauty, wonderment, and connectedness.

Meta Spiritual Principle

Present Tense Matters: Make a habit of living in the present tense, checking periodically for recurring *conscious participation required* experiences like laughter, play, beauty, wonderment, and connectedness.

9 – Relationships Matter

We humans have evolved to need connections with other people. We need each other to survive in the world.

Leave me naked and alone in some distant, out-of-the-way spot with no water, food, clothing, or shelter, and I am likely to die if someone doesn't rescue me.

I depend on other people for clean water to drink and nutritious food to eat. I cannot drill for oil or make gasoline. I understand how electricity is generated, but I need the help of others to power my home. I've never built a house, a car, or a highway, but, I need all three. And from time to time, I need the help of a doctor—even a hospital.

I am not alone in these dependencies. We all count on other people to stay alive.

We humans do not have the ferociousness of a lion or the strength of a gorilla. But we do have large brains, and one thing we have learned after tens of thousands of years is that we need each other. We have learned to survive by cooperating, sharing resources, and working together.

You don't have to be seeking spirituality in any form to

recognize the importance of transactional connections with other people—exchanges for food, clothing, shelter, transportation, and other necessities of life.

Meta-spirituality aims for the highest and best in life, and that includes how we view and participate in relationships.

Meta-spirituality calls us to engage in more than mere transactions with other people. It is concerned with how we can find depth and meaning in relationships.

Value Each Relationship for What It Is

For much of my adult life, my expectations were extremely high for every new friendship I made. I wanted all my acquaintances to be deep friendships—and I was often disappointed.

A light bulb moment occurred when a wise counselor challenged me to view each friendship, whether new or old, with a willingness to value it for whatever it could give—a glass half-full rather than half-empty approach.

If a friendship touched only one part of my life or the depth of conversations was not all I desired, I would choose to see the relationship as having value for what it offered, rather than rejecting or minimizing it because of what it did not provide. I would be grateful for what each friend was able to share, and I would be ready to give back.

This was a liberating concept for me: Don't expect every friendship to be the greatest you'll ever have—lighten up and be grateful for any human connection. It was liberating because it got me in sync with reality: Some relationships have more potential for depth, trust, longevity, and meaning than others. Small talk is not always a bad thing, and every positive human connection has value.

Accepting this truth did not stop me from placing priority on seeking and finding deeper relationships. And when I do find someone with whom I have an instant connection—someone with whom I can talk honestly about anything, someone who is usually on the same page as me, and even when they're not, somehow, we still connect—that is a serendipitous event for which I am especially grateful.

It's also true that not expecting too much of a friendship too soon allows it time to develop. What seems like a shallow relationship at first can turn into a deep one as two individuals learn to trust one another. Time, conversation, and shared events often allow this to happen gradually. Some close relationships hit the ground running, but most take time to grow.

All human connections have value, but high-trust, reliable, this-is-who-I-really-am relationships are priceless. We can increase the likelihood of developing such connections by practicing active listening, transparency, and accountability—and by connecting with one or more communities of like-minded people.

Engage in Active Listening

A basic tool for relationship building is the skill of active listening—a type of listening that "looks deeper." This is not a search for embarrassing truths or secret failures. This is about connecting with another person at a more profound level.

Learn to ask questions and to pay attention to the answers. Be curious about who the other person is, what they have to share, what is "beneath the surface," and what is unique about their story.

Think of active listening as a multi-sensory experience. Look for body-language cues. What is the emotional tone of the conversation? What is not being said? What facial cues point to a message between the lines? What emotions are you feeling as you listen?

When you practice active listening, you will find that you frequently walk away from a conversation with someone you've just met knowing much more about him or her than they know about you. But that's okay. What you will also find—eventually—are individuals who can reciprocate your level of interest, and that's how important connections with others can begin and grow.

Be Honest, Open, and Vulnerable

Deeper connections with other people will develop as we cultivate our skills for being honest, open, and vulnerable.

Emotional recklessness is not required. Personal

boundaries are important. We're looking for selected safe people who are worthy of our trust, and we need to remember that not everyone is trustworthy.

The first step is being a safe person yourself. Don't violate confidences. Be what you seek in others.

It's a good idea to become vulnerable with another person one step at a time. First, we can infer how someone will keep our confidences by how that individual talks about others. Then, we can share one "low cost" disclosure and watch for indications that the confidentiality is being honored. We can test the waters, so to speak, and allow time and multiple engagements with another person before we trust them fully.

If I share too much, and my confidant breaks our agreement by telling someone else what I've shared, I will let myself feel the pain, learn from the experience, and measure what I say to this person in the future.

Over time, we learn that one friend can be trusted at one level—with some limitations—while another friend can be trusted more. A few are worthy of unlimited trust.

Be cautious of someone who is ready for you to reveal all, but shows little or no personal vulnerability themselves. That's a warning sign.

Being honest, open, and vulnerable creates the possibility of emotional intimacy which is the key to a deep relationship of any kind. If I am unable to be honest and open about myself, if I am so afraid of being hurt that I am totally closed to everyone, I am an island. And I need to find, learn about, and address the source of my fear of self-revelation.[10]

Practice Accountability

A key aspect of meta-spirituality is taking responsibility for our actions. Choosing to be accountable is part of how we make sure that happens.

In the meta-spiritual view of human existence, there is no supreme being watching our actions; there is no concept of sin; and there is no life beyond this one. But none of this takes away a sincere concern for doing what is right. The difference is why we seek to do what is right and how we decide what is right and what is wrong.

Some values are cultural norms that are supported by laws and seem patently logical to most humans. Not a comprehensive list, but some examples are: Do not kill or physically harm another person, do not steal, do not violate another person's sexuality, and do not abuse other people, especially children, in any way—physically, sexually, or emotionally. Meta-spirituality acknowledges these commonly-held restrictions on human behavior, and calls for personal accountability to them.

Other values—ones that are seen differently even by different groups or sects within a particular religion—need to be worked out by each meta-spiritual individual. In the following chapters, I'll discuss some suggested core values for a meta-spiritual lifestyle, but here, my focus is simply on the idea of accountability.

Although we are not obligated to list and confess sins to a watching, potentially angry God, as required by some religions, we do need to practice accountability if we are to become our best selves.

Our efforts to do what is right will not be driven by fear, but rather by a desire to seek the highest and best in life. And we can't reach the highest and best in our behavior without accountability to other people.

Being accountable does not mean surrendering your personal boundaries, and it does not mean submitting to the authority of another person who is unopen to feedback from anyone else. Once again, we are looking for selected safe people.

We need to find trustworthy, like-minded confidants who will, at our request, lovingly, but honestly, tell us what they see in our actions. They will not limit their feedback to the good they see in us. They will call us to task when we have asked for feedback and they have seen us violating our values. They will speak the truth with courage and kindness as we make ourselves accountable to them.

Find Community

For people who don't believe in any supreme being, the primary source for understanding our world and how it works is science. And that is how it should be, but science does not provide the personal encouragement of a caring community.

Science provides the technology and medicine to treat you in the hospital, but science will not pay you a visit, hold your hand, and express personal concern. The discoveries of science will likely lead to a longer life than you would have known otherwise, but when you die, science will not attend your funeral service to eulogize you and say encouraging words to those you left behind.

Science can help you better understand what makes people—including yourself—who they are, but it will not offer you a communal group that helps you feel loved and accepted. Science—as far as I know—does not provide a weekly meeting where you can be encouraged to keep working on being a better person.

Meta-spirituality acknowledges our human need for the encouragement provided by like-minded people.

Without religion and faith, people can still benefit from organizations that "minister" to them. Churches and other religious congregations are about so much more than worshipping a deity. They implicitly understand that everyone needs to be connected to other people.

Free-thinkers may not be so dependent on a like-minded tribe as those who seek a religious authority to teach them what to believe in, but humans still need other humans, regardless of belief or lack of it.

Secular communities that meet weekly and mirror some of the same concerns as churches, synagogues, and mosques—but without reference to deity—now exist and are evolving in the U.S.[11]

The Houston Oasis is a Texas group founded by former pastor, Mike Aus, in 2012. This secular "church" describes itself as "a community grounded in reason, celebrating the human experience."[12] Out of the Houston group, a national organization called "Oasis Network" was formed. Here's how the Oasis Network describes its local groups:

> Oasis is a place for the non-religious to come together to celebrate the human experience. We understand that vibrant communities are central to human happiness and well-being. That's why we need Oasis: to provide a place for like-minded individuals and families to connect, be inspired and feel empowered.[13]

Another such group is the "Sunday Assembly." It was started in England in 2013, and now has chapters in eight countries. The organization's website states: "Why do we exist? Life is short, it is brilliant, it is sometimes tough, we build communities that help everyone live life as fully as possible."[14]

Opportunities exist to be in on the ground floor of helping

such groups emerge. The down side, at least for now, is that these groups exist in only a few cities. Hopefully, these secular communities will multiply and grow in the coming years.

For now, if you can't find a local tribe, you can connect across geographical lines, via online and regional groups and meetings. And you can learn the great value of even a few friends who see life in a similar way. A group does not have to be large to be your tribe.

Meta Spiritual Principle

Relationships Matter: Value each relationship for what it is, and do the things that enable relationships to grow. Engage in active listening. Be honest, open, and vulnerable. Practice accountability. Connect with a community. Always keep your boundaries in place.

10 – Values Matter

Do values matter if no God is watching and there is no life beyond this one? One could argue that if God is not real and life ends at death, there are no binding rules, and you can do whatever you please.

But laws, societal norms, and common reactions to certain behaviors still exist, even when you don't believe in God or an afterlife. And doing whatever you feel like doing—depending on what it is you feel like doing—may be barbaric, uncivilized, and illegal.

Theoretically, one could contend that the best strategy—when you believe neither in God nor in life after death—is to act like you are expected to act when others are watching. Then, when no one is looking, do whatever you choose, whatever feels good to you and advances your own interests—even if it includes things like cheating, stealing, or lying.

You could live this way, and some people do, but we have an ample supply of adjectives for them—double-dealing, deceptive, hypocritical, and insincere. Such people are inconsistent. We can't depend on them. They don't do what they say they'll do. They master a public persona that hides their true identity.

These individuals may push their way into positions of power, and can even win a misplaced respect from others, but, duplicitous, what-you-see-is-not-what-you-get people are not the kind of people you want your children to be. At least, I hope that's how you feel, because if it's not, you too may be broken.

Something goes wrong in us when we nurture a hidden identity that is drastically different from how we portray ourselves to other people.

I understand that any of us can find ourselves in a situation where some nuanced adjustment in our persona is temporarily made to deal with conditions that limit our options for responding.

I recognize that hard-to-shake societal expectations related to gender, ethnicity, and sexuality can often make it hard to fully express one's true identity. But these instances are not what I'm referring to.

I'm alluding to a person who consistently and willfully decides to act out a false identity as a way to control and manipulate other people. If you become such a person— even if your duplicity is not discovered—living your life is at least one component of your just punishment. If you're not a sociopath, then you have a conscience, and living with the constant cognitive dissonance that you create by being two different people is ultimately stressful and wearisome.

But my argument that values matter is not just that breaking the basic rules of life isn't smart, socially acceptable, or safe. It's not just that consistently and intentionally portraying a personal integrity that doesn't exist is dishonorable and emotionally exhausting.

The more important point is that when one stops believing in God and an afterlife, all inner impulses to be and do good, to respect the lives and property of other people, do not automatically disappear into thin air.

When I stopped believing in any religion or God, I didn't stop wanting to be a good person. I just had to figure out what being a good person looked like for me in my new approach to life.

I did stop believing it is necessary to pray multiple times each day—I stopped praying at all. I did cease observing Sundays as a day to attend worship services. I did stop looking to the Bible as the source for my core values. I did go through a period of evaluating what I believed about right and wrong—a relatively short, adolescent-like, trial-and-error phase that helped me decide where to set my new boundaries.

When the dust settled, my new list of core values did not look that different from my old one. I had not stopped wanting to become the best possible version of myself. I had not given up on a quest for value-driven living. And in many ways, I felt more genuinely myself—more authentic—than at any previous time in my life.

Not believing in God does not wipe out a desire to build character, a willingness to learn from mistakes, and a search for what is highest and best. And, the absence of faith does not automatically cause the moral quality of one's life to decline.

Our desire to be good and do good comes not from God, but from our evolved awareness that we need to cooperate with other people, from our childhood training, and from our life experiences. And it may also be genetic in ways we do not yet understand.

Every single day, all kinds of people who have no commitment to some other group's "one true religion" make choices to excel in their thoughts, actions, and relationships—and "all kinds of people" includes skeptics, agnostics, and atheists.

But what does character look like for the meta-spiritual person? While everyone must choose his or her core values, some common-sense guidelines apply. For example, while meta-spirituality is not a religion, and has no commandments, it recognizes the necessity of prohibitions against doing harm to others.

And a meta-spiritual core value doesn't really add up unless it has the potential to yield positive results for all types of people. It should not be racist, misogynistic, or bigoted in any way.

Meta-spiritual values may be borrowed and adapted from the religions of the world. Multiple religions teach us to treat other people as we would like to be treated. More than one religion calls for kindness, courage, giving, and gratitude. I choose not to argue with the honorable nature of such values.

In developing my own list of meta-spiritual core values, I've thought about what I learned from my former Christian faith—the personal values that still make sense. I've thought about principles that I saw practiced in support groups I led or participated in over the years, principles that helped people who were emotionally wounded or were struggling in some other way. I've thought about my own challenges to becoming a better person, and what has helped and hindered me. I've also thought about how balance is important, and I've attempted to keep things simple.

In the preceding chapters, I've presented some things that matter, and from these things that matter, I've started a list of meta-spiritual principles. Here's a summary of what I've shared so far.

Seeking Truth Matters: Look deeper, be willing to change your mind, and follow the truth wherever it leads.

Knowing Yourself Matters: Never stop learning about who you are—even when doing so is painful or challenging.

Recognizing Danger Matters: Don't give in to fear, but be realistic about life's dangers. Do what you can to protect yourself and others from harm.

Present Tense Matters: Make a habit of living in the present tense, checking periodically for recurring *conscious participation required* experiences like laughter, play, beauty, wonderment, and connectedness.

Relationships Matter: Value each relationship for what it is, and do the things that enable relationships to grow. Engage in active listening. Be honest, open, and vulnerable. Practice accountability. Connect with a community. Always keep your boundaries in place.

On the following pages, you'll find a discussion of seven core values, which, in my view at least, make sense for everyone.

Meta-Spiritual Principle

Values Matter: Build personal character on core values that work for everyone.

11 – Strength

People who are religious look to God for strength. They study their holy books, they worship, they obey commandments, they pray, they practice a sense of the presence of God in their lives—and through all these activities, they claim to receive a strength that comes *only* from God.

But since no personal, interactive God exists, any strength that follows the practice of such acts of religious faith comes from within the individual and from the encouragement of other practitioners of the faith—not from a benevolent deity.

Part of the meta-spiritual mindset is that we must find our own inner strength. We should not be afraid to look to family and friends for help in life, and we will, no doubt, find strength in their support. But we each need to recognize, build, and maintain our own inner core of strength.

Here's a good place to start. Think of a time in your life when you did something extremely difficult. Maybe it was standing up to an intimidating person. Perhaps it was working through a terrible loss in your life. Maybe it was walking away from a toxic relationship. Or, you climbed out of a financial hole and started over. Possibly, it was a marathon run, an educational achievement, or some other demanding goal you set and accomplished.

As you think about how you successfully managed this difficult challenge, loss, or trauma in the past, consider this question: Where did your strength come from?

Can you acknowledge that *you* were strong in the situation?

Can you concede that it was *your* strength that kept you going—even if others were helping you along the way? Decisions were made that only *you* could make. Actions were taken that only *you* could take. *You* took each step. *You* were strong.

Is it hard to acknowledge that you were strong at a crucial juncture in your life?

I spent decades listening to religious teachings telling me, over and over, that I was inherently weak and could only be strong with God's help. Credit for any achievement—large or small—was to be given to God alone, and I was constantly on the alert to not give too much standing to my own strength and resolve.

Life at home can inflict similar damage. If you grew up with a parent who constantly criticized, the negative words you heard countless times may still haunt you—and make it hard to see yourself as strong. Growing up with constant criticism makes it difficult to believe in your own value, insights, and strength.

When religious warnings or parental put-downs are echoing in your thoughts, acknowledging your own strength will be challenging—but challenging does not mean impossible.

I'm learning to visualize a core of strength within myself. I know that who I am is in my brain, and I know my brain is in my head, but—as unscientific as it may be—I find it more helpful when I imagine that my core of strength is in my gut. It's not logical. It just works for me.

When I feel disheartened, afraid, or overwhelmed, I visualize my inner core of strength. I remind myself of times in the past when I acted with strength, and I remind myself that I am tough.

I'm not Superman, but I am strong, and I'm guessing you are too—at least, you can be with the right mindset.

Strength Components

A bulging bicep is an obvious indicator of a type of physical strength. A triathlon medal testifies to the strength of physical endurance. But what are the signs of inner strength? What does inner strength look like? I'm proposing that inner strength has at least four key components: integrity, self-reliance, determination, and resilience.

Integrity

Integrity is about choosing to do the right thing regardless of the cost. It's also about being genuine and authentic in how you present yourself—a basic consistency in who you think you are, who you say you are, and what you actually do.

If integrity was easy, everyone would possess it, but it's not—there are so many things working against it.

Surrendering your integrity can be tempting when you're in a competitive environment with rule-breaking pressure from higher-ups.

When you do take a stand for what's right, and you're in the minority, there will likely be pressure to "let this one slide." But the one you let slide probably won't be the last one. You can expect future challenges to compromise, and if you keep "letting them slide," your integrity will slip away.

At times you may fear getting left behind. And this fear can tempt you to create another version of yourself—to embellish your story, your credentials, and your character.

It's easy to go with the flow, but if the flow takes a wrong turn—well, it's the flow, and you're in it. The exits are hard to find.

Living with integrity is a challenge, but not unattainable. We're not talking about perfection. It's normal to have some differences in your private and public personas. It's normal to look different than your best self when you're under tremendous stress.

It's also normal to make some mistakes. People with integrity sometimes make bad choices that violate their core values, and such lapses are characterized by varying levels of intentionality. When bad behavior seduces us, we're rarely completely unaware of what's happening, but when it's all over, we may still find ourselves sincerely asking, "How on earth did that occur?"

While not always true in the realm of public opinion, in the meta-spiritual view of things, you don't get just one chance at integrity. Authenticity can restart and resume when you acknowledge inappropriate behavior, take responsibility, make amends, and get back in sync with your core values.

Having integrity doesn't mean you never change directions.

As we experience life, learn, and grow, we gain new information that may lead to changes in values, goals, and purpose. Evolving in your identity is not the same thing as living with carefully constructed, multiple versions of yourself.

Integrity is a kind of wholeness. When lines of code in a software application are missing or corrupted, and the application stops working properly, the software is said to have lost its integrity.

Self-Reliance

Self-reliance is another component of inner strength. Being self-reliant doesn't mean you can't follow a leader, keep your opinion to yourself when appropriate, or let someone else take center stage. Self-reliance doesn't mean you can only work alone or that you never need help from anyone else. Being self-reliant doesn't mean you think you're always right, and believe everyone else is wrong.

Being self-reliant does mean you have developed an inner voice that says, "I can depend on me," and you refuse to let other people, institutions, or events define you or take control of your life.

Learning to stand on your own two feet doesn't mean you can't lean on someone else when you need to. It does mean that someone can lean on you without knocking you down.

You can be self-reliant as an introvert or an extrovert, female or male, old or young. It's not about age, gender, or personality type. It's about knowing who you are, being grounded by your integrity, and taking responsibility for the direction of your own life.

At the same time, developing self-reliance and having it recognized by others may be more challenging based on your gender, age, or personality type. For example, self-reliance may be valued more if you're male than female. And if you've been expected to be dependent all your life—regardless of the reason—developing self-reliance will likely be a challenging task that requires extra effort, but if you are determined enough, you can still do it.

Determination

Determination is the third component of inner strength. Determined people persist and stay on course, even when a hundred things get in the way. Determined people see obstacles as problems to be solved. And if they do get sidetracked, their determination soon has them back on course.

Determination is what you need when giving up looks inviting. As is true with integrity, being determined—to get where you want to go, to reach your goals, and to see your dreams come true—does not mean you never change. A mid-course correction is not the same as giving up.

Determined people do things that have never been done before—like sending astronauts to the moon or developing a new drug for stroke victims. Determination sends a firefighter into a burning building to save someone when it looks like an impossible task. Determination takes an Olympic athlete to world-class levels of performance.

Determined people do "small" things too, things you don't read about in the newspaper, but feats that are good news to the individuals they affect. Determined people are not always loud and standing at the front of the room. Theirs may be a quiet determination that escapes attention, but nevertheless, gets the job done.

Determined people have a positive impact on the lives of

people they teach, coach, counsel, parent, inspire, lead, and befriend.

A determined attitude is well set on a foundation of integrity and self-reliance. But when determination meets its match, when things fall apart, and starting over is the only option, one other component of strength is needed.

Resilience

Simply stated, resilience means getting up when you fall down. We all have it when we're toddlers. Toddlers fall down all the time. Sometimes they cry, but they always get back on their feet. They accept falling down as part of their normal routine, and that's how they learn to walk.

In adult life, resilience means you always find a way to start over after experiencing a setback or loss—no matter how discouraging, debilitating, or tragic it was. Resilience means you can adapt when the floor falls out from under you. If you have to, you find a way to learn new skills, to start a new career, to make a better attempt at marriage—whatever it takes to start over and rebuild.

When life backs you into a corner and has almost convinced you there's no way out, resilience allows you to change your thinking, your attitude, and your behavior—and get going again.

Resilience means you can live in the present because you refuse to get stuck in the pain, the irony, or the indignity of past losses and mistakes.

Strength and Courage

Courage is the willingness to do something you know you need to do regardless of how frightening it is—and that requires strength.

Strength and courage feed one another. You need strength to be courageous, but each time you act with courage, you get a little stronger.

When you add courage to the strength of integrity, self-reliance, determination, and resilience, you can see dramatic results. You can stand up for what is right, even under pressure. You can do things you never thought possible. You can persist when others give up. And you can bounce back when everyone thought you were done.

Strength Training

The question is: How do you build inner strength?

Do What You Want to Become

Life teaches us that the way to get better at something is by doing it—over and over—and learning from your trial-and-error experiences.

Practicing integrity builds integrity. Choosing an attitude of self-reliance—in one situation after another—builds self-reliance. Persisting in persistence builds your determination muscle. Getting up—one more time—when you have fallen down in life, builds resiliency.

You get stronger by being strong—one situation at a time.

Challenge Yourself

You can increase your physical strength—over time—by regularly lifting progressively heavier weights.

Inner strength is no different because it too increases as you push yourself beyond what is easy.

Here's a good place to start. Do something you are afraid to do. I'm not recommending bungee jumping or sky diving. Keep safety in mind, but choose to do something that could fail, something that challenges you, something you really want to do, but are afraid to do.

Maybe you decide to take a class in public speaking. Maybe it's taking a trip on your own. Maybe you finally sign up on that dating service. Maybe it's deciding you're willing to chair a committee you serve on.

It can be something than anyone else would consider a trivial matter, but to you, it's not—it's a challenge because it's something you fear.

You may or may not succeed in your first attempt, but either way, you will be moving away from fear. And you can always learn from your mistakes, and try again until you get it right.

If you succeed—wonderful! If not, don't think of your activity as a failure. Instead, let your response to the outcome be your measure of success. Pat yourself on the back for giving it a go, then challenge yourself again.

Never Stop Learning

"Look deeper" and "never stop learning," are meta-spiritual concepts that apply here. Learning increases knowledge, and knowledge makes you stronger.

Become an avid student of your own distinctiveness. Learning about yourself, your gifts, your blind spots, and the areas where you need to grow are all important.

In your quest for knowledge, self-awareness is the launching pad. Cultivate a curiosity about all kinds of things. Learn all you can about what makes other people who they are.

Observe. Listen intently. Ask questions.

Increase your awareness of all that surrounds you. Learn all you can about your work, your family, your culture, the world, the universe.

This isn't about comparing your learning power to someone else's. It's about getting out of auto-pilot mode, looking at life with more curiosity, and paying more attention to what you see.

The payoff: Knowledge decreases helplessness. Knowledge makes you stronger.

Strength Awareness
If you have a recurring tape in your brain that keeps telling you how weak you are, we need to replace it immediately!

I would like you to begin right now in thinking of yourself as a strong person, and here's how to get started. It's something I mentioned a few pages earlier—thinking back to times in your life when you were strong.

Think again about occasions when you did something that was extremely difficult—things like standing up to an intimidating person, working through a terrible loss, walking away from a toxic relationship, climbing out of a financial hole, or completing a challenging task like an educational achievement, a marathon run, or some other hard-to-achieve goal you set for yourself.

As you think about these times in the past when you acted with inner strength, pick the event that moves you the most when you remember it. Which memory evokes the greatest emotional response? Create a mental picture of yourself at that moment in time when you were strong. You might morph this mental picture into an imagined logo for your own inner strength.

Think of this mental image often and use the memory of the strength you displayed in this past event to help you really see yourself as a person with a core of inner strength, a person who is growing stronger day by day.

Meta-Spiritual Core Value

Strength: Visualize your inner core of strength, and practice strength training to build integrity, self-reliance, determination, and resilience.

12 – Kindness

Kind is not a word you would normally look up in a dictionary, but if you did, you would find multiple synonyms—words like affectionate, benevolent, caring, considerate, friendly, generous, gentle, helpful, sympathetic, and warm.

I'm up for being on the receiving end of all these traits as often as possible. Aren't you?

I want my life to intersect with kind people. It's a no brainer.

I consider myself a kind person, and would like to think I'm always as ready to give kindness as I am to receive it.

But sometimes, my selfish side gets in the way. Sometimes I'm tired. Sometimes I'm not paying attention. And some people are harder to be nice to than others.

Even when kindness is part of our DNA, we still need to work at it. We still need to make the effort to improve our kindness quotient—our ability to be kind to all types of people in all kinds of situations—it's part of the effort to find our best selves.

Components of Kindness

It's helpful to know what we are aiming for as we seek to display more kindness. I'm focusing on four components.

Respect

Treating another person with respect is a form of kindness. Respecting someone doesn't mean you agree with them—you don't even have to like someone to show them respect.

A measure of humility is helpful as we attempt to show respect for other people: their existence, their space, their boundaries, their rights, their property, their time, their privacy, their struggles, their experience, their views, and where they are in their own journey.

After my convictions first changed from faith to non-belief, I went through a period of intolerance for people who still believed the things I had believed for most of my life. Gradually, I recognized the need to be more accepting. Today, when I meet a person of faith who can neither understand nor respect my current lack of belief in any religion or God, I try to see the former version of me in that individual—something that helps me to be more tolerant and to communicate respect.

Even when someone is vastly different from any past or present version of me, even when I have no way of relating to how they view life, I can still choose to be tolerant and respectful.

There are limits. I do not require myself to respect the

behavior of abusive people. I will not respect hateful ignorance, racism, or other kinds of intolerance.

I can choose—with full confidence in the quality of my character—to avoid or confront such people and attitudes. In these situations, strength and courage may be more important than kindness. But I want to be cautious and reluctant about making the decision that avoidance or confrontation are the only options available.

Empathy

Before I label someone as beyond hope of change, beyond growth, beyond responsiveness to acts of kindness, and worthy of avoidance or confrontation, I want to put myself in their shoes. Trying to see how things look through the eyes of someone I'm interacting with—empathy—is a component of kindness.

The starting point for understanding how another person sees things is listening—without judgment.

If I can attain some small measure of success in seeing things through another person's eyes, I may understand that individual's position better, and I may find more inner strength to show the kindness of respect.

It's more than understanding another person's views on politics, religion, or life in general. Empathy is about trying to understand how another person feels given the situation they are in. It's about thinking of what I would need or want if I were in the same state, but's it's more than that. It's about trying to learn whether this person needs are the same, similar, or different than what I would need.

And sometimes, empathy means a willingness to help even when the help is not merited, to show respect when it may not be deserved, to be supportive when it would be okay to say, "You're on your own."

Patience
Patience is an expression of kindness, and a by-product of empathy. As I understand someone better, I may find it easier to be patient with their behavior.

If patience were a traffic sign, it would read "Slow."

Patience is about decelerating to a slower pace because someone else needs me to. Saying yes to patience is saying no to a driven pattern of thinking, a racing mind, and the constant feeling that I'm running late. Slowing down allows us to listen better, to get onto the same page, to really connect.

Children need our patience. Spouses and partners need our patience. Aging parents need it. People who are hurting need our patience. And we need to learn to be patient with ourselves.

Forgiveness
When we have been hurt or betrayed, when it's hard to see anything good about how someone has treated us, respect,

patience, and empathy may not be enough—forgiveness may be the only way of moving forward.

Forgiving another person is an act of kindness—toward the other person, but also toward yourself. You do yourself a favor when you let go of the weight of resentment and the negative feelings that accompany it.

I can think of things I've done that probably did not deserve forgiveness, but the offended person chose to forgive me anyway, and I'm deeply grateful. I want to be the kind of person who forgives even when I could convince myself that the other person doesn't deserve it.

Forgiveness does not mean the offensive act was acceptable. I can forgive someone and keep my boundaries on alert if I see indications the offense may be repeated. I may even choose to distance myself for protection, but I can still forgive.

In the course of our reasonably healthy relationships, forgiveness will be a two-way street, a way of coping with our human imperfections, our bursts of self-centeredness, and our occasional fearful need to take charge of things that are not ours to control.

Forgetting how someone wronged you may not be possible since it's hard to control what we forget. However, forgiveness is an act that can enable a relationship to continue when it would have otherwise ended.

Kindness With Strength

Kindness works best in partnership with a confident inner strength. Something's missing if you're kind only because you're afraid to be any other way.

Courageous kindness sets and maintains personal boundaries. It says no to being victimized or taken advantage of by others.

If you're interacting with someone who regards kindness as weakness, your strength and your boundaries are what they need to see.

And sometimes you need to stand your ground not because the other person is an abuser or a bully, but just because it's important for the other person to know where you stand. Sometimes the kindest thing you can do for another person, and for yourself, is to be strong enough—and courageous enough—to speak the truth, even though it's painful for you and for the person you are speaking to.

At other times, the strongest, most courageous thing you can do is to kindly choose silence when everything in you wants to shout your frustration, fear, or pain.

Meta-Spiritual Core Value

Kindness: Keep building your kindness quotient as you practice respect, empathy, patience, and forgiveness, while remembering that kindness works best in partnership with a confident inner strength.

13 – Truthfulness

We humans have learned to survive by cooperating, sharing resources, and working together—all activities that require effective communication.

Truthfulness is what makes communication work. Lying—the distortion, replacement, or strategic omission of accurate information—damages the value of language, and can lead to a failure to communicate.

When communication breaks down, whatever human endeavor it is supporting deteriorates, whether it is a business deal, peace negotiations, or a close relationship.

The meta-spiritual mindset is concerned not only with finding out what is true, but also with telling the truth. And it sees truthfulness as one of the basic building blocks for positive and productive human interactions.

Truthfulness is the foundation for meaningful trust in all relationships. It's the basis for the emotional intimacy that occurs when you develop a close relationship that has depth, meaning, and resilience.

As imperfect humans, we all fudge on the truth

occasionally. The niceties of social interaction can create grey area conflicts between politeness and truthfulness. A quick response in a stressful moment—upon later reflection—may reveal itself to have been less than truthful.

Adopting truthfulness as a meta-spiritual core value does not mean we are aiming for perfection, but it does mean we are aspiring to make our truthfulness habitual.

Truthfulness is a foundational character trait, a reference point for the kind of person you are, and a way that others decide whether they can count on you.

If you're known for not telling the truth, you have a serious handicap—you cannot be trusted. And if you can't be trusted, this gap in your character will affect your work, your friendships, and your deepest, most important connections with other people.

From a logical standpoint, truthfulness makes sense. So, why is lying so frequently a tempting choice?

A lie is a shortcut—an easy way to get through an awkward moment, and a convenient avoidance technique.

We lie to avoid embarrassment. We lie to avoid facing consequences of previous actions. We lie to avoid what we don't want to do. And sometimes, we lie to manipulate.

But telling a lie is like taking out a loan you can't pay back.

Lying erodes trust. It damages, and sometimes, ends relationships.

It's telling that even liars don't like to be lied to—the reasons: accurate information is crucial to whatever you are undertaking in life, and being lied to feels devaluing.

Lies are used to avoid, hide, and confuse. A lie points you right when you should go left. A lie creates anxiety when there is nothing to worry about. A lie convinces you to let your guard down just when you should be alert.

Not every lie is an act of evil, but according to author and psychiatrist Scott Peck, where evil is present, you will find lying.[15]

Truthfulness is tied to the strength of integrity. Truthfulness requires courage. This is about where we aim, and when it comes to telling the truth, we need to aim high.

How we tell the truth is also important. Truthfulness is no excuse for a lack of kindness. Tone, timing, and discretion apply to how we tell the truth. And with those we love, truth should never be weaponized, but should be delivered with gentleness and care.

Meta-Spiritual Core Value

Truthfulness: Tell the truth with strength, courage, and kindness.

14 – Humility

Humility is an elusive target. No matter how hard you work to attain humility, you can never claim you've achieved it.

"I've mastered humility," doesn't sound like something a humble person would say. It sounds like something an arrogant person would say, and arrogance is the opposite of humility.

Humility is a virtue best attributed to you by someone else—and not your public relations person. If you think you're humble, you should keep it to yourself.

And how do you work at being humble?

One of my friends, in a sincere effort to be humble, would never accept a compliment. Rather, he would downplay or deny the significance of any accolade sent his way. The result: The one giving the praise would repeat it with even greater enthusiasm—sometimes more than once—trying to make sure the compliment was properly delivered and received.

My friend's sincere effort at humility backfired, and drew

more attention to himself. Trying to be humble can be like trying to forget something—the more you think about it, the more you remember it.

And, how much humility is enough? If striving for humility is not your own idea—if it's an externally imposed command or preachment—it's easy to feel guilty for not being humble enough just when you are at a point of healthy self-esteem. A guilt-driven effort at humility can become a whack-a-mole hammer poised to smack down any sense of healthy pride about a meaningful accomplishment.

So, how can we attain a virtue so elusive as humility?

One way is to focus not on attaining humility, but on keeping a healthy perspective. We can go outside on a clear night and ponder the stars. We can think about the massive size of the universe, our short tenure on this earth, and the limited impact any of us will have on the grand scheme of things.

Maybe we are fortunate enough to have some positive impact on a few of our contemporaries. And some of us will manage to make contributions that outlive us. If we are parents, our children are likely to be our best contributions to the future. But despite all our efforts, each of us is so miniscule and—in reality—insignificant.

This awareness can be discouraging, even overwhelming. It could lead you to decide that nothing you do has any significance, and that all your efforts—along with life itself—are meaningless.

I must admit that I liked it better when, as a Christian, I thought my actions had consequences in another life beyond this one. I liked it better when I thought this life on earth was the blink of an eye compared to an eternity in heaven. I liked it better, but what I used to believe is not true.

Not only are we tiny specks in the world, but there's so much we don't know. Some subjects are complete mysteries, and are likely to remain that way as long as you and I live.

I choose not to be overwhelmed by the awareness of how insignificant my life is in the big scheme of things, and by the scope of the things I'll never know. I choose to let this awareness be a source of humility.

A realistic perspective of one's place in the universe leads to a natural kind of humility as opposed to the forced attempt at a virtue commanded by some authoritative source. This is a kind of humility that allows self-esteem and says it's okay to feel proud of a job well done.

I choose to say yes to aiming for this kind of humility.

One of the benefits of this type of humility is an openness to new ideas. Humble people are better at admitting what they don't know, and an awareness of what we don't know can enhance a thirst for new information, insights, and learning.

An open mind can foster a receptiveness to encounters with a diversity of people who may become the source of previously unimagined perspectives.

The opposite of an open mind is a closed one. Close-minded people build rooms with no windows. Close-minded people fear what new ideas will do to their beliefs, their self-esteem, and their ways of coping with life.

Close-minded people are arrogant. Arrogance says things like, "Of course I'm right" and "You don't know what you're talking about."

Arrogance is unattractive. Arrogance is a wall.

Humility is admirable. Humility is an open door.

I vote for humility, but don't ask me if I'm humble. Ask me if I'm working to keep a good perspective on who I am in the whole scheme of things.

Meta-Spiritual Core Value

Humility: Humility is the opposite of arrogance, and it's about keeping your perspective on who you are in the whole scheme of things.

15 – Gratitude

One of the most natural expressions of humility is gratitude. Gratitude is a way of admitting that you are not the source of everything good in your life.

After I left my faith, I remembered something I had read when I was still a minister: "Thanksgiving is the hardest holiday for non-believers because they have no one to thank."

It was a put-down, a taunt to non-believers, and I used it in a Thanksgiving sermon after reading it. Decades later, my rejection of faith put me on the receiving end of this condescending idea, but I decided that was okay.

Admittedly, gratitude for life and all the good it brings is harder to aim without a personal deity to thank, but that doesn't mean a meta-spiritual person can't be grateful.

I feel tremendous gratitude for the gift of life itself. I'm extremely thankful for the good things about life that I can't really thank other people for, things like: the beauty of a sunny day, the cozy melancholy of a rainy afternoon, the drama of a lightning storm, the wonder of the Grand Canyon, the grace of the birds that fly over the small lake behind my house, and so many, many other things. I feel grateful for all these "gifts" without needing to identify a specific source for them.

The same is true of my gratitude for the good fortune of having family and friends, my thankfulness for the positive things that happen in my life, and my sense of—for lack of a more secular expression—being richly blessed. My level of gratitude is not hindered at all by the lack of a personal God to thank.

In fact, in my Christian life, I felt obligated to be grateful. The Bible commanded me to be thankful, and sometimes I felt that I could never be thankful enough. Sometimes I felt guilty that I was not more grateful.

In the meta-spiritual mindset, I do not practice gratitude in obedience to a directive from a religious book. Any thankful attitude that I now hold is spontaneous and unprompted. It's not an obligation—it's a natural response, a voluntary feeling—and I like that.

And of course, gratitude includes expressing appreciation to other people. Saying "thank you" is such a basic part of our interactions with others.

The meta-spiritual way challenges us to be creatively articulate in our expressions of gratitude to other people. A phone call just to say thank you, a special gift, an intense look in the eye when verbally thanking someone—all have the potential for memorable expressions of gratitude.

Being grateful is a good way to live.

Virtually every book or article I've read about how to be happy includes gratitude as one of the ingredients, but even without those confirmations, the value of gratitude is self-apparent.

Gratitude is about treating others the way we would like to be treated. Who doesn't like it when someone else shows their appreciation? And what kind of people don't say thank you? Bullies and other rude people, self-centered people, and people who lack social awareness.

If you give something to a small child and a parent is present, you can assume the parent will quickly remind the child to say thank you. It's basic training.

An instantly understandable put-down of another person is to say he or she is an ingrate—something no one wants to be called.

As you work on keeping a good perspective on who you are in the whole scheme of things, gratitude will come more easily, but it still requires effort.

Meta-Spiritual Core Value

Gratitude: Remember that you are not the source of everything good in your life, and make a habit of expressing gratitude for all the good that comes your way.

16 – Generosity

According to the Gospels of the New Testament, Jesus taught his followers to go the extra mile—to give more than what was commonly expected—to go beyond reciprocity.

In my decades of service as a minister I did see many Christians going the extra mile, giving more than they received, and attempting to display a servant attitude toward others—just as Jesus taught.

To keep things in perspective, these same Christians believed God would reward them for their faithfulness. Believers see faith in Jesus as the pathway to heaven, but the validity of one's faith is shown by actions. And acts of goodness—like generous sharing of time, talents, and money—were expected to be a VIP badge of honor for believers in the life to come.

If there is no personal God evaluating our lives, is there any reason to go the extra mile—to step beyond reciprocity—ever? Is there any reason to be generous or to give to people who have nothing to give back?

Does giving more than we receive make sense when there is no afterlife—no ultimate balancing of the scales where we will be compensated for the times we gave more than we got?

I say yes. Generosity still makes sense.

Think of the concept of going the extra mile as it applies to relationships. For instance, which do you think works better in a marriage or life partnership—a relationship in which each partner is careful to give 50 percent but no more, or a relationship in which each partner gives 110 percent? If you're not sure of the answer, ask two or three couples in long-term, successful relationships what they think.

The same is true in just about any kind of relationship whether it is a friendship or a business connection. Going the extra mile is not only admirable, but it feels good and frequently yields greater benefits in a multitude of ways.

And I think it's telling that even people who are not generous themselves frequently admire people who are.

Do we admire such behavior because a deep part of us senses that giving more than you get is the best way to live, that this is life on a higher, nobler plane?

When I was very small, one of my aunts gave me two pennies to buy two pieces of round chewing gum from a vending machine full of multi-colored, sugar-laden gumballs. I placed the first penny in the slot, pushed the lever to the left until the machine clicked, and out rolled a red gumball, making a metallic sound when it hit the little swinging door that kept it from falling to the floor.

As I opened the door, pulled out the gumball, and put it in my mouth—while preparing to insert the second penny to buy another piece—I noticed a boy, slightly younger than me, standing nearby. He was looking longingly at me and at the gumball machine.

I placed my second penny in the slot, pulled the lever, and gave him the second gumball, which, upon seeing him, I had quickly decided I didn't really need.

My aunt, observing what happened, grabbed me by the arm, and pulled me aside. She bent down to look me right in the face and said, "No, no, don't do that. Be stingy!"

I must have been four or five years old at the time, but something deep within me knew that what she was saying wasn't right. I felt no guilt from her words, and I felt good about sharing my second penny, far better than having two pieces of gum to chew.

Even as a child, I felt strongly that sharing was a good thing to do. Maybe I had learned it in Sunday School. Maybe I had learned it from my dad. One of his cousins told me that my father was the kind of guy who would give you the shirt off his back.

Or maybe it was just something that children innately understand before they learn to fear not having enough.

Sincere generosity conveys a certain confidence, a victory over the fear of not having enough—an anxiety that I'd better hold on to everything I've got or I'll end up with nothing.

Giving without an expectation of a reward or return seems like a noble thing to do. Even without a divine reference point, it seems right and good—a natural expression of confidence, humility, and gratitude.

The meta-spiritual view of generosity is opposite that of the self-made individual who looks at someone who is less successful and says, "I worked my way up the ladder, and you could too if you really tried." I'm sure that sometimes, that statement is true, but consider the following comparison.

Imagine a child born to two emotionally sound, physically healthy, well-educated, financially-secure parents. This child comes into the world with good health, a high IQ, a likeable disposition, a lean body type, and an attractive face. The child is multi-talented, athletic, energetic, has leadership abilities, enjoys people, and is highly optimistic. And all these traits are apparent by the time the child is five years old, if not sooner.

Now imagine another child born to a single mom who did not finish high school and became a mother at the age of 15. This mom was abused as a child, lives on welfare, is diabetic, and her IQ is under 100. This mom suffers from chronic depression, has low self-esteem, and no one, even her mother, ever told her she was special in any way.

We know that the way life works, either child could turn out to be a smashing success or a colossal failure by any one of several standards of measurement. Some individuals squander great opportunities, while others overcome tremendous odds. It happens every day.

It's also true that life will be more challenging for the child born to the single mother on welfare than for the child born into the affluent, healthy, two-parent family.

The point is that we don't all begin life at the same starting line. Some of us have a head start, while others are going to have to work very hard—probably needing lots of help along the way—just to get to the point where others begin.

When we have a good sense of our place in the big scheme of things, when we realize that we don't all begin at the same starting line, and when we understand how lucky we are for the starting point we received, generosity is a natural choice. It's another expression of humility, and it's a way of showing gratitude for the good that has come our way through no efforts of our own.

For the secular person, there is no invisible God to whom we feel an obligation to give, but there are plenty of living, breathing persons who need help, and to whom our generosity can be directed.

Generosity will often need the test of balance, especially

in our ongoing relationships. The meta-spiritual model is giving generously in relationships while using one's self-awareness to know when you are giving too much or too little.

If I consistently find myself in relationships (or organizations) in which I am always giving, but not receiving much in return, I need to examine why this is the case. I will also need to work on boundaries.

A simple boundary is contained in the following response to a request to help, volunteer, or rescue: "No, I'm sorry, that's not something I can do right now." Notice the response begins with the word "no."

Some people and some organizations operate like vacuum cleaners that will suck the emotional life out of you if you let them. Setting boundaries on how often you see or talk to toxic people and setting boundaries on your involvement with any organization that won't stop asking you to give more and more is a good thing.

If the toxic person is a family member or some other irreplaceable person in your life, the challenge is to set boundaries that allow you to be the whole person you seek to be. For other relationships, discontinuing the toxic connection may be the best option.

Involvement in an energy-draining organization needs to be evaluated in the same manner as with an energy-draining individual.

Here's another checkpoint: If you are willing to give, but not willing to receive, that's a warning light for control issues. If you're always on the giving end, there's a reciprocity imbalance, and you have the power—the recipient is likely to feel some uneasy form of obligation to you. If giving is easy, but receiving is difficult, figure out why, and aim for the balanced state of giving *and* receiving.

The other side of the equation is that sometimes we may not give enough. If you constantly find yourself in relationships and organizations where you are receiving, but giving little or nothing back, self-analysis is in order. Is there a part of you that is afraid to let go, to give generously, and to trust the results? Have you unconsciously—somewhere along the way—gotten comfortable with being a taker and not a giver?

I think generosity is an important core value and a good way to live, but it's your choice. In a religious environment you will likely be commanded to be generous. Not so in the meta-spiritual realm.

Meta-Spiritual Core Value

Generosity: Aim for generosity, but remember that you get to decide how generous you want to be.

17 – Love

You don't have to love someone if you don't want to. If your response is, "Everybody knows that," you've probably never been religious.

I lived 50 years of my life committed to my Christian faith. The number one commandment—made clear in words attributed to Jesus—is to love God with all your heart, mind, and soul. It was an impossible goal, but it's what I tried to do.

Over those years, I expressed my love for God by attempting to follow the ethical guidelines of my faith, by studying to learn more and more about God, and by faithfully attending church.

My love of God was in response to what I believed was his love for me. I saw him as my creator, my loving heavenly father. And, he sent his only son—who was both separate from him and the same as him—to die for my sins.

My sense of a call to ministry at the age of 16 was a response to the call of a loving God, and it was a commitment to spend my life sharing God's love with other people.

For decades, I worshipped God, I served God, and I prayed to God—and the basis for all of it was showing my love for the God who loved me first.

Christians are commanded not to worship idols—human-made sculptures that represent a deity—and it was easy to preach about the foolishness of primitive religions in which people pray to a silent statue made of stone.

In the end, for me, relating to the God of my faith wasn't much different than talking to a stone god. How can you be in a loving relationship with an invisible, silent being you've only read about in a book?

Participating in religious services with other Christians, and in my case, leading such services, did generate a sense that something was there, something we could all feel.

A congregation of devoted believers singing heartfelt songs of faith made what we all believed seem more real, more present, and more palpable. I remember one song often sung as a solo in church, and it repeated—over and over the words: "My God is real. My God is real."

We didn't need songs that said, "My spouse is real" or "My car is real." But we did need a song that said, "My God is real," because none of us could see or hear God in any normal way.

We needed to get together and stir ourselves up with song and sermon to stoke the fire of our faith.

You're probably only minutes away from some person who will assure you on a moment's notice that "My God is real, and I feel his presence in my life every day." I understand that sense of faith, but I also know that whoever makes such a statement has never heard the voice of God in a way that moves an eardrum, and has never seen God in a way a camera could record.

When I left my faith, one of the ways in which I felt a sense of relief was in no longer needing to pretend to be in a loving relationship with a God who is silent and invisible—just like a pagan idol.

Religion teaches children and adults to love someone they can't see whether they want to love him or not. And if they don't love the invisible God by whatever name he, she, or it is called, they're in trouble. It's crazy thinking: "Love God like he loves you, or you will be punished!"

You don't have to love a God who isn't there, but what about love for other people? Isn't it a little odd to have a list of core values that doesn't include—as the first item on the list—an imperative to love other people?

How about this? Follow the relationship guidelines suggested in the preceding pages. Practice the core values of strength, kindness, truthfulness, humility, gratitude, and generosity in relationships and see when, where, and with whom love happens. My money is on love being the fruit of meaningful human connections that grow out of the practice of these guidelines and values.

So, instead of imploring you to love, I implore you to be kind—and kindness includes respect, empathy, patience, and forgiveness. I commend the value of truthfulness that is measured out by kindness. I encourage you to find the strength and courage to keep your commitments, live by your values, and overcome your fears. Choose humility. Practice gratitude. Be generous. And let love happen naturally.

Can you imagine a person who practices all of these meta-spiritual principles not being a loving person? I can't.

I like the idea of love happening not as the result of an imperative, but rather as the natural consequence of who we are and the natural outcome of all the other traits of meta-spirituality that we practice.

This is a liberating concept: You don't have to love someone if you don't want to. My old religious self gives me a jab when I write those words, but I'm going to ignore the jab and stick with the concept: You don't have to love someone if you don't want to.

Meta-Spiritual Core Value

Love: Let love happen naturally. You don't have to love someone if you don't want to. Just remember to be kind to everyone as much as humanly possible.

18 – Purpose Matters

Spiritual people find meaning and purpose in God, his promises, and his plan for their lives. Meta-spiritual people find their own meaning in life by discovering and following a value-driven purpose in life without reference to God or religion.

Recognize the wonderful freedom you have to decide what is important to you. If you are not sure, follow your best guess and see how it works. If your first try does not work, follow your intuition, and try again.

Consider your search an adventure. With your core values in mind, keep looking until you have a sense—at least a tentative one—of what your passion is. Follow your passion to find your purpose. Pursue your purpose to find meaning.

Meta-spirituality sees purpose and meaning as more important than happiness.

Our level of happiness will rise and fall with life events. Some days will feel better than others. Sometimes happiness is not appropriate for what is happening in our lives. Sometimes we need to hurt. Sometimes we need to grieve. Sometimes we need to struggle. Meta-spirituality calls us to own and process whatever we are feeling. It calls us to allow what we have no control over to happen. It echoes the conviction of the Serenity Prayer in regard to accepting what we cannot change.

One thing we can seek no matter how happy or unhappy we feel at a given moment is to be fully engaged in doing what feels fulfilling.

The positive psychology movement has given us the concept of flow, which refers to the sense of being so involved in what you are doing that you become unaware of the passing of time. When you are in this state of energized focus, you may look up and say, "I can't believe two hours have passed."

We have more control over experiencing flow than we do over feeling happy.

Happy is wonderful. I hope for as much of it as I can get. However, if my own happiness is all I seek, I will often fail. I will frequently feel empty.

Instead of constantly trying to be happy, consider focusing on what you are passionate about. Focus on what energizes you.

Before writing this book, I worked with a life coach to make a course correction. I wanted to reflect on the work I was doing. I wanted to be sure I was following my passion. I wanted to review my core values. I wanted to reassess my purpose. The result: I determined that my current purpose is to help others find insights that lead to personal growth.

Writing this book is tied to my sense of purpose. Writing these words feels meaningful. Sometimes, writing is exasperating, but most of time when writing, I feel a sense of flow, an energized focus. Time passes quickly. I'm likely to continue until I just can't write any more.

Working on what I know is my purpose has a smooth feeling about it. When you follow your passion, there is a self-propelled energy involved. That doesn't mean it's never frustrating or discouraging, but it does mean that—most of the time—it feels good when you're doing it. And when it doesn't feel good, it's still worth the effort.

Time flies when you are having fun, but time also flies when you are living out what you have discovered to be a meaningful, value-driven purpose for you, something you are passionate about, something that makes life flow.

Meta-Spiritual Principal

Purpose Matters: Meaning comes from pursuing a value-driven purpose you are passionate about.

Part IV – How to Keep Moving Forward

Expectancy Matters

Dead Weight Matters

Pacing Matters

Inspiration Matters

Self-Care Matters

19 – Expectancy Matters

Phrases like the daily grind, the nine-to-five routine, and the treadmill of life complain of a sense of being trapped in an endless, recurring cycle.

While it's true we can never escape certain repetitive aspects of life—waking, eating, bio breaks, sleeping, and starting over the next day—we can learn to embrace a larger view.

The grander view is seeing life as a journey—a trek in which one thing is certain—we need to keep moving forward. The alternatives are being stuck in a hamster cage, or worse, moving backwards to an earlier state, sinking into depression, and watching life pass us by.

Some of life's most meaningful moments can happen while you're standing still, sitting down, or when you're flat on your back. But to have a sense of meaning that goes beyond mere moments, a fulfillment that is more consistently present—we need a sense of moving forward.

We can teach ourselves to see life as an exciting expedition, not a straight-line trip from here to there, but rather, an exploratory journey with countless stops, side trips, and multiple course corrections along the way.

Sometimes our destinations will be planned targets on our route—places we've worked long and hard to reach. But we'll also discover lovely spots we didn't know existed—surprising places that demand more than a moment's attention to soak in all they have to offer. And sometimes we'll need to stop for repairs.

The fuel for forward movement in this journey is a sense of expectancy—the idea that no matter how difficult or great life has been so far, something to look forward to lies ahead. It's the hope that some out-of-the-blue, wonderful thing could be just around the corner. It's a readiness for a new idea, event, or person that will lead to unexpected enlightenment, growth, or joy. It's the sense that something good is going to happen.

Believing the best is yet to come is a natural when you believe in life after death, but looking for eternity can also be a way to miss the value of the here and now. In the meta-spiritual view of things, we do not expect an existence beyond this one, but we can still choose to believe that the best is yet to come.

This is all another way of saying, "Don't give up hope."

I want to be careful that this does not come across as a callous disregard for people whose lives do—in a realistic and objective way—feel hopeless. Some people need a life preserver thrown to them. Some people need help from those of us who are not drowning.

Regardless of how bad things are for you, I still say, "Don't give in to hopelessness." I know it's easy for me to say, and I know that life is not always fair. But I also know that if any one of us gives in to hopelessness, we can sink so deep into the darkness of despair that we may not see the outstretched hand of opportunity when it is offered.

My Christian belief system told me that no matter what happened, no matter how bad it seemed, I could have faith that God was working through it for my greater good. Meta-spirituality makes no such promises. I don't actually know if anything good lies ahead, but I choose to expect that good things will happen.

Sometimes bad things happen with no good elements in or around them. But one thing that is near impossible to take from us is the decision to look ahead with hopeful expectancy.

In a meta-spiritual world, *hopeful expectancy may be the closest thing we have to faith.* Let this expectancy gently pull you forward in your journey.

Meta-Spiritual Principle

Expectancy Matters: Choose to believe that something unexpectedly good lies ahead. You're more likely not to miss something good if you're looking for it.

20 – Dead Weight Matters

Whether you're on a long hike or running a race, one thing is certain: you don't want to be lugging extra weight.

If you're hiking the Appalachian Trail, you'll make sure your backpack isn't too heavy before you take the first step. If you're a sprinter in a track meet, you'll wear minimal clothing—lightweight clothing at that—and you'll be wearing shoes designed to be as light as possible.

Regardless of your mode of self-powered movement, more weight requires more energy, and it makes no sense to carry anything that slows you down.

It doesn't matter how fast or far you're going. Carrying an unnecessary load is a disadvantage, and if the load is too heavy, it can slow you down to a snail's pace—or stop you altogether.

I'm not referring to loads measured in pounds. I'm referring to psychological burdens like toxic shame, obsessive guilt, unreasonable fears, consuming envy, and chronic hatred—dead-weight overloads for life's journey.

Toxic Shame

It's helpful to think of guilt as being about what you've done, and shame as being about who you are.

Shame isn't all bad. The ability to feel shame keeps us from walking down the street with no clothes on. It makes us care about social graces. The capacity to feel appropriate levels of shame marks us as civilized humans.

Chronic shame that hangs around for the sole purpose of making you feel bad about yourself is toxic, and it's one of the types of dead weight we need to shed.

If you were shamed over and over again in your formative years, or if you took on the shame of an emotionally unhealthy parent who would not own their own shame, you may have emerged from childhood with a shame-based identity.

Shame can be worn in different styles. In one mode, the shame-based individual says, "I'm sorry" an awful lot, and may seem ready to apologize for even existing. On the other end of the spectrum, a shame-based person may act shamelessly—in defiance of the hidden tormenter. For still others, the shame may be invisible to everyone but the person who lives in it.

When you're shame-based, you may repeat shaming behavior that was modeled for you, and make a habit of blaming others. Shame and blame are a powerful, destructive duo.

Shame is a burden we can reject, but it will take some work if shame has been drilled in deep. Don't hesitate to seek the help of a counselor or support group to break shame's grip on you, if that's what you need.

A simple, but powerful, starting point for breaking free of toxic shame is the phrase: "I give you back your shame." It's meant to be uttered silently when you're being shamed by someone else and want to shake it off.

When I completed my book, *Goodbye Jesus*, and was about to release it for publication, I was completely sure of the assertions I had written on the subject of my disbelief. I was not plagued by a fear that the God of my former Christian faith might be real or that hell might await me as an apostate. And yet, I felt twinges of shame for the book I was about to make public. My parents and all my aunts and uncles were deceased, but I could imagine one of my aunts saying, "What would your mother think? How could she deal with your not being a Christian anymore?"

Toxic shame is not logical, and the shame I felt about my dramatic change of beliefs, about my becoming part of something I had always condemned in the past, was no exception.

Toxic shame is a raw emotion, and it's not unlike a case of indigestion. It's just there, uninvited and unpleasant.

The release of my book was an opportunity for me to practice what I teach—to say to my religious past: "I give you back your shame."

Obsessive Guilt

Healthy guilt is a reminder to correct your mistakes. When you take the appropriate actions after doing something wrong, healthy guilt goes away. Like toxic shame, obsessive guilt is not solution-oriented, and it wants to hang around no matter how you respond to it. It exists simply to make you feel bad.

As a Christian, I believed that Jesus had died for my sins. In one sense, this was good news because it meant that all my sins—past, present, and future—were forgiven. In another way that may be hard to understand if you have never lived in this mindset, having received salvation from Jesus was also a reason for constant watchfulness for sin.

Though in one sense completely forgiven, I still needed to be aware of sins going forward, confess them to God, and ask his forgiveness. This was about maintaining my day-by-day connection with God, not about avoiding hell, since that was already taken care of.

One of the results of this mindset for me, and for anyone else sincerely committed to this kind of belief system, was that at any given time, cognizant of our human tendency to err, you had to assume you had committed some sin in the last 24 hours—even if you couldn't remember what it was. This had the potential for making you feel a constant need to confess something to God even if you couldn't remember a specific sin you needed to acknowledge.

In the world of Christian faith, the more you care about pleasing God, and the harder you try to be obedient, the more likely you are to be conscious of your failings.

Nominal believers don't worry as much about such things.

In the meta-spiritual view of life, we don't have sin. We don't have a God who is recording our every mistake. We don't have religious authorities who are cataloging and ranking lists of disobedient actions and thoughts.

Meta-spirituality recognizes the value of healthy guilt that calls us to corrective actions, and we have a sense of accountability to society, family, co-workers, community members, friends, and to ourselves. But obsessive guilt, in the meta-spiritual view of things, is dead weight that needs to be tossed aside.

When we are heavy with legitimate guilt and need absolution, we will have to find our own version of a priest. It may be a counselor, a family member, or a friend. We can admit our failures, talk about them, and somehow, in the admission of how we've failed, in our willingness to talk about what we did wrong, and in our readiness to make amends, we can experience a lifting of the burden of guilt.

Unreasonable Fears

A certain amount of fear helps us stay alive. It's a good thing that the idea of walking across a freeway blindfolded is frightening. It's not bad if you're afraid to see just how fast your car can go on a rain-soaked, winding country

132   A Meta-Spiritual Handbook

road in the dark of night. If you're on a hike, and come to a stream that is obviously dirty and polluted, a fear of drinking the water is in order.

But there is a kind of unhealthy fear that magnifies danger, and becomes a dead weight that can wear you down. The phrase "crippling power of fear" is applicable. Fear can immobilize you.

Imagine this. I place a steel beam, 12 feet long, 24 inches wide, and 12 inches high on a concrete floor. I offer you $1,000 to walk the 12 feet from one end of the beam to the other. Will you take me up on my offer? Of course, you will! It's easy money.

After you walk the beam and collect your prize, suppose I snap my fingers and, magically, a hole—10 feet wide and three stories deep—appears under the steel beam. It's the same beam, just as wide and just as long, but it straddles a deep pit. Will you go for another $1,000?

It's the same beam, and—in one sense—the difficulty of walking across it has not increased, but the consequences of falling have changed. You can surely walk across the beam again—if you do not let fear distract you. But that's easier said than done because fear can make it more likely that what you are worried about will actually happen.

A good starting point in dealing with unreasonable fears is talking to yourself about the things you fear. "What is it that I am actually afraid of?" "When did this fear start?"

"What is my fear really about?" "What can I do to move beyond my fears?"

Get help if you need it. Make up your mind that you will do whatever it takes to overcome the dead weight of unreasonable fears.

Consuming Envy

Unless you're the richest, best looking, most powerful, and most admired person in the world, it's hard to go through life without feeling some envy. And even if you are all those things, you may still find yourself feeling jealous when your closest competitors are nipping at your heels.

When things you've worked hard for, but have not attained, come easily for someone in close proximity, it's hard not to feel a twinge of envy. Maybe we can't avoid some feelings like this.

A greater concern is consuming envy, a kind of jealousy that keeps you focused on wishing for someone else to fail.

If you are wallowing in jealousy, you've probably stopped feeling grateful, and you may have lost any semblance of humility. And, it's to be expected that your jealousy is taking away from a healthy and positive focus on moving forward in your own life without regard to anyone else's pace or progress.

Consuming envy is another kind of dead weight, and it's related to one other dangerous burden: chronic hatred.

Chronic Hatred

We can make a case for hating evil if such hatred empowers us to combat evil in an effective way—we could even call this feeling righteous indignation.

But what about hating people simply because they are not "your kind." What about chronic hatred of people because of skin color, religious preferences, gender, or any other arbitrary descriptor? What about hatred that is fueled by jealousy? What about hating someone just because you don't like them?

What's wrong with hating someone if there is no God, no sin, and no ultimate judgment? The answers are simple.

Chronic hatred is an energy burner. Chronic hatred is a form of arrogance. Chronic hatred loves your fears. Chronic hatred is dead weight.

Meta-Spiritual Principle

Dead Weight Matters: Travel light by letting go of toxic shame, obsessive guilt, unreasonable fears, consuming envy, and chronic hatred. Get help if you need it.

21 – Pacing Matters

It may seem strange after what I've written in the preceding pages, but I'm compelled to begin this chapter with a verse from the *King James Bible*.

> But they that wait upon the Lord shall renew their strength; they shall mount up with wings as eagles; they shall run, and not be weary; and they shall walk, and not faint.
> Isaiah 40:31

Don't worry. I haven't reverted to preaching, and I'm not advocating that you learn how to wait on the Lord. It's still the secular me addressing you.

Sometimes, Bible verses communicate accurate truths about life that transcend the book's supernatural message. Isaiah 40:31 is a good example as it describes four states in regard to movement—stationary (waiting), walking, running, and flying. These four travel states provide a good model for our *moving forward in life* metaphor.

One key to continued forward movement in life is not running yourself into the ground. The way to avoid burning out is to pace yourself. Pacing matters.

I would not want to run through an art exhibit. I don't need a jet to get to the grocery store. I wouldn't want to try to walk from Texas to Europe. And if I'm in a foot race, I don't want to be standing still. In other words, different modes and speeds are appropriate for different situations.

When you experience a great loss in your life—a death, a divorce, a career failure, or any other severe cause of grief, you'll need to sit for a while. You'll need to stop to regain your bearing. You'll need to pause to feel your emotions. These are healthy things to do—normal when working through a loss.

Then, as the shock and numbness wear off, you'll be accomplishing a lot to get out of bed each day and do the normal things you need to do. You'll be in a walking mode. When you've experienced a great loss, and you're just getting back into your routine, it's an accomplishment to keep putting one foot in front of the other.

Eventually, with enough time and enough processing of your grief, all options for forward movement will be back on the table.

Sometimes, you'll be in a running mode. You're working toward a goal. You're excited about it. You're pushing hard, and all the lights are green. Run, run, run! The finish line looks good.

Every now and then, if you're lucky, you will feel like you're flying—a child is born, one of your dreams comes true, something happens that exceeds your wildest expectations, or everything you touch turns to something better than it was. Soaring feels good.

And sometimes we crash. We aim too high and we fall. We run too far and we collapse in exhaustion. These are times when life is telling us we must stop and recharge.

We need balance in our travel modes. This includes seeing our meaningful "standing still moments" as part of our forward movement. Taking time to stop, to focus on our breathing, to meditate, to practice mindfulness—these are travel skills.

Mindful waiting is part of the desired pace for living. Meta-spirituality does not wait on the Lord. Meta-spiritual waiting is about having patience—not needing to have everything make itself clear, happen, unfold, or gain closure right now. It's about learning to trust the process of planting seeds and letting them grow. It's about sitting quietly, listening to your own breathing, and finding peace in the moment.

We each have our own kind of inertia. Some of us have trouble getting started while others have a hard time not running everywhere we go. Some of us need a little heat under the seat to get us going, and some of us need help in slowing down. Our challenges at pacing will be different depending on what our inherent inertia state looks like.

Regardless of your natural bent, you will need to think just enough about the past to learn from it and to be sure you are free of it.

You will need to think just enough about the future to know where to aim and how to plan for it.

But you will always need to remember that where we are right now—this moment—is the most important place you will ever be, because NOW is when and where life happens.

Meta-Spiritual Principle

Pacing Matters: Pace yourself in life's journey—walking, being still, running, and flying—all have their place, and remember that NOW is when and where life happens.

22– Inspiration Matters

The ability to be inspired is a key quality of spirituality in any form. And leaving faith does not mean leaving inspiration behind. We just have to be open to finding it in more diverse ways.

Not long ago, I watched news footage of Elon Musk's rocket pushing into space, launching his Tesla convertible into orbit—one more phase toward developing a spacecraft that will fly to Mars. It felt like another giant step for mankind, and I was inspired.

But accomplishments don't have to be headline worthy to inspire us. We can be inspired by anyone who beats the odds, overcomes seemingly impossible obstacles, and just won't give up. I love stories of people who do things family, friends, and peers never thought they could do. Such accounts inspire me to face my own challenges with strength and to live my life with courage.

We can also be inspired by our interactions with nature. We can be inspired by great works of art, by music, and by the stories told through books and film.

I recently watched the movie, *The Post*, an account of the

owner and editor of *The Washington Post* grappling with a decision of whether to publish classified material about the Vietnam War in 1971—information they felt the public needed to know. It was an issue of freedom of the press. The owner and the editor of the paper risked legal charges and prison if they published the information, but they did it anyway.

At one point in the movie, as the final decision to publish was being made, I couldn't keep the tears from welling up in my eyes. I was inspired by the courage and commitment of *The Washington Post* team to making sure American citizens knew the truth about the war.

What inspires you? What brings a tear to your eye and a lump to your throat? Stay alert for such things, whatever they are. When you're inspired, it's easier to take the next step forward.

Meta-Spiritual Principle

Inspiration Matters: That which inspires us breathes life into us and helps us to keep moving forward. Inspiration touches the core of what makes us able to be spiritual.

23 – Self-Care Matters

This life is all we have. The calendar years measured by your birthdays are not preparation for another life that begins when this one ends. When you die, everything is over.

Your brain is your life. It holds your memories, your hopes, and your dreams. Your brain is providing you with the sense of this present moment as you read.

There's no hidden, invisible soul—your body is you.

Taking care of your body, and especially the brain that runs it, is of utmost importance.

So, it makes sense to educate yourself on how you need to eat, how you need to sleep, and the kind of exercise you require. It makes sense to put what you learn into practice.

Nobody's perfect. Do the best you can. Work with what you've got. Strive for some level of consistency. Don't beat yourself up. When you get off track, get back on.

Become the world's best authority on what your body and brain need for optimum functioning.

Treat your body like a priceless, irreplaceable automobile you've been given to keep your whole life—with the understanding that you cannot get another one.

If you need to go to a doctor, pick the best one you can find and afford, and go. If financial problems make medical help seem out of reach, become relentless in your search for someone who will help you. Don't give up.

If something's broken and it can't be fixed, be as positive as you can about it. Find your own unique ways to keep moving forward in life.

Meta-Spiritual Principle

Self-Care Matters: Take care of your body. You won't get another one, and you can't keep moving forward without it.

Part V – How to Practice Meta-Spirituality

Reality, Meaning, and Movement

Inward, Upward, and Outward

Brokenness, Rebuilding, and Beauty

24 – Reality, Meaning, and Movement

The first step toward practicing meta-spirituality is reviewing—on a regular basis—its key concepts. Let's start the process right now with a review of the principles and core values described in the preceding chapters under the headings: "How to See Reality," "How to Live With Meaning," and "How to Keep Moving Forward."

How to See Reality

Meta-spirituality is about seeking truth and wanting to understand things as they really are.

Seeking Truth Matters: Look deeper, be willing to change your mind, and follow the truth wherever it leads.

Knowing Yourself Matters: Never stop learning about who you are—even when doing so is painful or challenging.

Recognizing Danger Matters: Don't give in to fear, but be realistic about life's dangers. Do what you can to protect yourself and others from harm.

How to Live With Meaning

Meta-spirituality yearns for what is highest and best in life, and meta-spiritual people find meaning by living in the present tense, placing value on relationships, and honoring their core values as they pursue a chosen life purpose.

Present Tense Matters: Make a habit of living in the present tense, checking periodically for recurring *conscious participation required* experiences like laughter, play, beauty, wonderment, and connectedness.

Relationships Matter: Value each relationship for what it is, and do the things that enable relationships to grow. Engage in active listening. Be honest, open, and vulnerable. Practice accountability. Connect with a community. Always keep your boundaries in place.

Values Matter: Build personal character on core values that work for everyone.

> **Strength:** Visualize your inner core of strength, and practice strength training to build integrity, self-reliance, determination, and resilience.

> **Kindness**: Keep building your kindness quotient as you practice respect, empathy, patience, and forgiveness, while remembering that kindness works best in partnership with a confident inner strength.

Truthfulness: Tell the truth with strength, courage, and kindness.

Humility: Humility is the opposite of arrogance, and it's about keeping your perspective on who you are in the whole scheme of things.

Gratitude: Remember that you are not the source of everything good in your life, and make a habit of expressing gratitude for all the good that comes your way.

Generosity: Aim for generosity, but remember that you get to decide how generous you want to be.

Love: Let love happen naturally. You don't have to love someone if you don't want to. Just remember to be kind to everyone as much as humanly possible.

Purpose Matters: Meaning comes from pursuing a value-driven purpose you are passionate about.

How to Keep Moving Forward

Meta-spirituality teaches us to see life as an exciting expedition, not a straight-line trip from here to there, but rather, an exploratory journey with countless stops, side trips, and multiple course corrections along the way.

Expectancy Matters: Choose to believe that something unexpectedly good lies ahead. You're more likely not to miss something good if you're looking for it.

Dead Weight Matters: Travel light by letting go of toxic shame, obsessive guilt, unreasonable fears, consuming envy, and chronic hatred. Get help if you need it.

Pacing Matters: Pace yourself in life's journey—walking, being still, running, and flying—all have their place, and remember that NOW is when and where life happens.

Inspiration Matters: That which inspires us breathes life into us and helps us to keep moving forward. Inspiration touches the core of what makes us able to be spiritual.

Self-Care Matters: Take care of your body. You won't get another one, and you can't keep moving forward without it.

Although this summary of meta-spirituality is only a few pages long, it's still a lot to remember. And practicing meta-spirituality is more than learning what it means. There's one more thing we need.

25 – Inward, Upward, and Outward

L et's construct a simple statement that sums up meta-spirituality in a couple of lines—a meta-spiritual mantra—something that is not only a short reminder of what meta-spirituality teaches, but is also a tool for implementing it in day-to-day living.

Meta-spirituality is about seeking truth and wanting to understand things as they really are—this requires that you **dig deep**.

Meta-spirituality yearns for what is highest and best in life, and this requires that you **aim high**.

The practice of meta-spirituality focuses on always remembering that where you are right now—this moment—is the most important place you will ever be, because NOW is when and where life happens. So, it makes sense to **find your best self in the present moment**.

Finding your best self in the present moment doesn't mean you only think about "now." Sometimes your best self in the present moment is a self that is reflecting on and learning from past experiences. Sometimes your best self in the present moment is a self that is considering what steps toward growth can be taken tomorrow or next month or next year.

Dig deep. Aim high. Find your best self in the present moment. And there's one more thing.

Meta-spirituality reminds you to **connect**. It challenges you to fully engage with the richness of human relationships, the joys of life's beauty and wonder, and the helpful resources that are available to you.

When you recognize the significance, value, and power of connecting, it makes sense to frequently check your connections. "What connections in my life are broken, and what can I do to repair them?" "What new connections are waiting for me?" "What connections do I need to initiate or plan?" "Am I missing a positive connection that is begging to happen?"

Now we have it. Here's the meta-spiritual mantra. **Dig deep. Aim high. Find your best self in the present moment. Connect.**

I find it helpful to talk to myself using this mantra, or some part of it, in a way that applies to whatever challenge I might be facing.

If I'm having a difficult conversation with a person I love,

I can say to myself, "Find your kind and caring self in the present moment. Don't let hurt or anger break this connection, even temporarily."

If I'm interacting with a sales or service person and notice that my mind is somewhere else, I can challenge myself, "Find the part of you that values relationships at every level. Initiate a friendly connection."

When life looks dreary and feels exhausting, I can tell myself, "Self-resuscitate. Find the you that loves laughter, beauty, and play. Do something that will pull you into the goodness of life in the present moment."

If I'm feeling toxic shame, I can say to myself, "Dig deep. Find your shame-free self in the present moment. Connect with the emotional healing work you've done."

When I'm feeling afraid, I can say, "Dig deep. Aim high. Find your courageous self in the present moment. Connect with your inner core of strength."

If I'm having trouble getting on task, I may tell myself, "Find your purposeful self in the present moment. Connect with the why behind the task."

If I'm having trouble slowing down, I can tell myself, "Dig deep. Find your quiet, calm, and peaceful self in the present moment. Connect with your breathing."

At other times, I may just remind myself of the mantra or

a part of it. I may tell myself, "Find your best self in the present moment," or "Connect," or "Aim high," or "Dig deep."

If you want to make the principles and core values of meta-spirituality a driving force in how you think and live, I recommend that you re-read this chapter and the preceding chapter frequently. And I recommend that you use the meta-spiritual mantra often.

Another helpful resource can be found at www.Meta-Spirituality.com/Reminders.aspx. There, you can sign up for a program that will email, text, or phone you with random reminders of meta-spiritual, principles, values, and mantra suggestions.

26 – Brokenness, Rebuilding, and Beauty

Years ago, I read about a church somewhere in Europe that was bombed during World War II. The most memorable part of the hollowed-out church building had been a stunningly beautiful, stained-glass window. In the days after the bombing, members of the church picked up the pieces of the shattered window and hid them away.

When the war was over and the church was rebuilt, an artist was hired to create a new stained-glass design using the tiny broken fragments from the original window. When the artist's work was finished, everyone who saw the new window said it was more beautiful than the one it replaced.

After my life of faith collapsed, I picked up the broken pieces and tried to envision a new way of seeking the highest and best in my life. It took me years to think through what still matters to me, and this book is the result of that process.

If nothing else, this is a handbook for how I want to live my life, but I hope it is more. I hope that somewhere in these pages, you have found something of value and beauty that will help you seek what is highest and best for your own life.

Other Matters

Feedback Requested

About the Author

Endnotes

Feedback Requested

If you've found this book helpful and would like to encourage others to read it, you can make your voice heard by writing a brief customer review on Amazon.com.

Login to the Amazon account you used to buy this book. Type "meta-spiritual" in the search box at the top of the page, then press the Enter key. Next, click on *A Meta-Spiritual Handbook's* cover image from the list that appears below the search box. When the book's Amazon page opens, scroll down to find and click the Write a Customer Review button.

Click on the number of stars you want to give the book, then a box will appear where you can write your comments. Your review doesn't have to be eloquent or lengthy. Type in a few sentences that will help someone like you decide whether the book would be helpful to them. When finished, click the Submit button and you're done.

Thank you in advance for your feedback.

About the Author

Tim Sledge is a humanist writer and speaker whose mission is discovering and sharing insights for personal growth. You can read his latest articles and stay in touch via his website, MovingTruths.com.

Sledge is a former Southern Baptist pastor and author. After devoting his career as an evangelical preacher to leading and growing ministries in Illinois, Tennessee, New Jersey, and Arizona, he moved to a suburb of Houston, Texas, where, as senior pastor, he led his church to experience dramatic growth and wrote two books that launched a ground-breaking support group ministry. *Making Peace with Your Past* and *Moving Beyond Your Past* have now been in print for more than 20 years, and have been used as interactive guides for 20,000 support groups across the U.S.

At the peak of his ministerial career, a 10-year series of events led to a growing awareness that faith was no longer working for him. His journey into and out of faith is described in his book, *Goodbye Jesus*.

Endnotes

[1] David Richo, *How to Be an Adult in Relationships* (Boston: Shambhala Publications, 2002), 4.

[2] Robert Fulghum, *All I Really Need to Know, I Learned in Kindergarten: Uncommon Thoughts on Common Things* (New York: Ballantine Books, 2004), 10.

[3] If no such personal acquaintance is available, consider a qualified professional counselor, and commit to enough sessions to make yourself known. You'll be surprised at the insights that become available to you within a few sessions if you are honest, open, and vulnerable. Don't let the lack of funds deter you. Be proactive. Some counselors will occasionally work with a client for a dramatically reduced rate as an act of service. Community counseling services may be available. If you cannot find a counselor, look for free support groups that can offer help.

[4] "Latest Crime Statistics Released: Increase in Violent Crime, Decrease in Property Crime," FBI Website, September 26, 2016. https://www.fbi.gov/news/stories/latest-crime-statistics-released

[5] Martha Stout, *The Sociopath Next Door: The Ruthless Versus the Rest of Us* (New York: Broadway Books, 2005).

[6] Marie E. Rueve and Randon S. Welston, "Violence and Mental Illness," Psychiatry MMC, May 2008, online article: https://www.ncbi.nlm.nih.gov/pmc/articles/PMC2686644/.

[7] "Alcohol Use Disorder (AUD) in the United States" and "Alcohol Related Deaths," National Institute on Alcohol Abuse and Alcoholism, https://www.niaaa.nih.gov/alcohol-health/overview-alcohol-consumption/alcohol-facts-and-statistics, citing A.H. Mokdad, J.S. Marks, D.F. Stroup, and J.L. Gerberding, "Actual causes of death in the United States 2000," [Published erratum in: *JAMA* 293(3):293–294, 298] *JAMA: Journal of the American*

Medical Association 291(10):1238–1245, 2004. PMID: 15010446.

[8] "Child Abuse Statistics & Facts," *Childhelp*, citing C.W. Harlow, "Prior Abuse Reported by Inmates and Probationers," Washington, DC: US Dept. of Justice, Office of Justice Programs, Bureau of Justice Statistics, 1999. https://www.childhelp.org/child-abuse-statistics/?gclid=EAIaIQobChMIiJL4w-3Q2AIVBbnACh1yrwxiEAAYAyAAEgIkQPD_BwE.

[9] M. Scott Peck, *People of the Lie: The Hope for Healing Human Evil* (New York: Simon and Schuster, 1983), 223-226.

[10] If this is the case with you, consider finding a qualified professional counselor who can help you with a plan for developing new relationships with people who are emotionally safe, people with whom you can be honest, open, and vulnerable. Don't let the lack of funds deter you. Be proactive. Some counselors will occasionally work with a client for a dramatically reduced rate as an act of service. Community counseling services may be available. If you cannot find a counselor, look for free support groups that can offer help.

[11] Adam Lee, "Why People Are Flocking to a New Wave of Secular Communities: Atheist Churches, https://www.alternet.org/belief/why-people-are-flocking-new-wave-secular-communities-atheist-churches, November 27, 2013.

[12] "About Us," Houston Oasis Website, https://www.houstonoasis.org/about-us.

[13] "About Oasis," Oasis Network Website, https://www.peoplearemoreimportant.org/about-oasis.

[14] Sunday Assembly Website, https://www.sundayassembly.com/story.

[15] M. Scott Peck, *People of the Lie: The Hope for Healing Human Evil* (New York: Simon and Schuster, 1983), 242.

Made in the USA
Monee, IL
14 June 2021

71194202R00100